2,000 NEW LAUGHS FOR SPEAKERS

The Ad-Libber's Handbook

ALSO BY ROBERT ORBEN

Ad-libs
Best of Current Comedy
Big, Big Laughs
Bits, Boffs and Banter
Boff Bundle
Calendar Comedy
Comedy Fillers
Comedy Jackpot
Comedy Quickies
Comedy Show-Stoppers
Comedy Technique
Crack Comedy
Current Comedy Sampler
Emcee Blockbusters
Emcee's Goldmine
Emcee's Handbook
Encyclopedia of Patter
Exclusive Comedy File
Flip-Lines
Gag Bonanza

Gag Showcase
If You Have to Be a Comic
Laugh Package
M. C. Bits
Magicdotes
One-Liners
Patter for Standard Tricks
Patter Parade
Professional Comedian's
   Source-Book
Professional Patter
Rapid-Fire Comedy
Screamline Comedy
Sight Bits
Spotlight on Comedy
Tag-Lines
333 Belly Laughs
Working Comedian's
   Gag-File

Complete Comedian's Encyclopedia—Volume One
Complete Comedian's Encyclopedia—Volume Two
Complete Comedian's Encyclopedia—Volume Three
Complete Comedian's Encyclopedia—Volume Four
Complete Comedian's Encyclopedia—Volume Five
Complete Comedian's Encyclopedia—Volume Six

The Joke-Teller's Handbook or 1,999 Belly Laughs

2000 New Laughs for Speakers:

The Ad-Libber's Handbook

BY ROBERT ORBEN

GRAMERCY PUBLISHING COMPANY
NEW YORK

Dedicated to Stan and Viv Kupferman

This book was originally published under the title
The Ad-Libber's Handbook: 2,000 New Laughs for Speakers.

Copyright © MCMLXII, MCMLXIII, MCMLXIV, MCMLXV,
MCMLXVI, MCMLXIX by Robert Orben
All rights reserved.
This edition is published by Gramercy Publishing Company,
a division of Crown Publishers, Inc.,
by arrangement with Doubleday & Company, Inc.
    c d e f g h
GRAMERCY 1978 PRINTING
Manufactured in the United States of America

Library of Congress Cataloging in Publication Data

Orben, Robert.
2000 new laughs for speakers.

Originally published under title: The
ad-libber's handbook.
1. Public speaking—Handbooks, manuals, etc.
2. American wit and humor. I. Title.
[PN4193.I5073 1979]   817'.008   78-10647
ISBN 0-517-26600-8

INTRODUCTION

There are several thousand joke books on the market. They contain several million jokes. More accurately, they contain a few thousand jokes, stated in several million ways. They contain bons mots, stories, witticisms, and are bulked up with quotations from Mark Twain, Voltaire, and Shakespeare. Most of them have one thing in common—they are not of this era.

The modern communicator, be he pro or amateur, must speak to the subjects of his day. Drolleries of the nineteenth century do not work with modern audiences. Humor has to match the tempo of the present time—fast, short, incisive. Subjects have to be the concerns of people today—space travel, Southeast Asia, color television, demonstrations, the Pill. Topicality is the essence of the "now" humor. A joke must have all the impact and timeliness of an ad-lib.

The purpose of *The Ad-Libber's Handbook* (as well as its predecessor, *The Joke-Teller's Handbook*) is to provide you with more than 2,000 of these laugh-getters, conveniently classified so that you can drop one into any part of a talk, presentation, or performance where humor is called for. Thoroughly absorb the contents of these books and your reputation as a "spontaneous" wit will soar.

A few suggestions for the nouveau quipster:

Don't do any joke unless you are sold on it yourself. It is frightening enough to get up in front of an audience without adding the further burden of doubting your material. When reading through this book for the first time, put check marks beside the items you enjoy and feel are compatible to your personality. Rely on this first impression because there is always the tendency to question the worth of a joke or series of jokes as the time for performance draws near. If you liked it the first time, chances are the audience will too.

Relative to this thought, don't try to read this handbook as you would a novel. Too much humor at one time is like eating a pound of chocolates at one sitting. Only the first few jokes or chocolates are truly appreciated. Read a few pages at a time, rest, and then return to it. You will find yourself in a better frame of mind to judge the material, and your ability to unconsciously retain some of the jokes will be increased.

When putting the material to use, even if your knees are knocking, your hands are clammy, and your heart is pounding with fright—try to look as if you're enjoying yourself. An atmosphere of fun and confidence is essential to the effective telling of a joke. If you seem to be at ease and enjoying the experience, this communicates itself to your listeners.

Speak the way people speak. Many platform performers acquire a pompous manner and an artificial delivery the minute they stand in front of a microphone with a pitcher of water beside it. Keep your tone conversational and your words and sentence construction completely natural. To help you in this, the jokes are written in a colloquial (oops, down-to-earth) style that most people would feel at home with.

Personalize the jokes whenever possible. When doing a medical joke to a group of doctors, make sure the doctor in the joke is a well-known member of your audience. Localizing a story will always increase its effect.

Look at your audience—in the eye. One common, albeit ineffective, way to cope with stage fright is to stare at the back wall, or ceiling, or space, and pretend that the people aren't really there. This lack of focus gives your eyes a glazed look and is just another barrier to a feeling of oneness between you and the audience. As you deliver the material, keep looking at different people and look them right in the eye. If nothing else, at least these few will feel obligated to react.

Use your imagination when considering the material in this book, and review the subject matter from time to time. Many of the political jokes have an underscore in place of a name so that you can just drop in the current applicable personality. Entire categories may have a multiplicity of applications. For instance, there is a category entitled Peyton Place. As this is being written, the TV series is in its final season of shooting new shows. It will, however, be on television for many years more via reruns and syndication of its present shows. Beyond this, Peyton Place has become a generic term for a small town where anything can happen. The next time such a real-life small town makes the headlines, all your Peyton Place material comes alive again.

When you've told your joke, have the courage to wait for your laugh. Don't immediately rush into your next sentence to fill the silence. The reaction to a joke told by a professional comedian is usually much faster than to one told by a speaker in the midst of an otherwise serious speech. It takes the audience a little while to assess the fact that a joke has been told and then to assess the joke itself. So wait and give them a chance to enjoy.

One final note of advice: If they don't laugh within two minutes after the punch line—to hell with them. They had their chance.

BOB ORBEN

CONTENTS

11

A

ADVERTISING

One of the nice things about Christmas in a big city is the way office buildings leave lights on at night to form a cross. And you can always tell the buildings on Madison Avenue. They're the ones with the double cross.

It may be the way the cookie crumbles on Madison Avenue, but in Hong Kong it's the way the egg rolls!

I know a biologist who's gone Madison Avenue. Keeps talking about tired lymph.

It's no wonder we're having so much trouble. All over the world countries are guarding against Communism, subversion, nuclear attack—and what are we guarding against? Tooth decay!

Have you ever seen that phrase: GUARD YOUR TEETH? I just found out who's behind it. A company that makes locks for water glasses!

There's a brand-new tooth paste on the market that really gives you a feeling of confidence. It tastes like a dentist's fingers!

Now they've got a new deodorant that's so effective, people don't even know you're around. It's called VICE-PRESIDENT!

I just bought that new razor blade that gives you the world's closest shave. Operates on an entirely new principle—from the inside!

As far as I'm concerned, these supersharp blades are worth every cent they charge for them. Yesterday my wife tried to cut the linoleum with one of them. Went right through to the cellar!

13

You can always spot the fella who gets eighty-two shaves from a single blade. The blood bank follows him around with a bucket.

They say Dr. Frankenstein is very interested in that bread that builds strong bodies eight different ways.

AVOID HOME ACCIDENTS! What a great slogan for Planned Parenthood.

I just thought of the perfect impasse: Avon calling and Revlon answering!

It's kinda sad—like finding an old copy of *Collier's*—and the very first ad is for an Edsel.

Did you hear about the madam who decided to use modern merchandising methods? So she's calling her place: GERT'S RENT-A-TART.

AIR CONDITIONING

Personally, I don't think they should rate these air conditioners by B.T.U.'s but by decibels. You work one whole summer beside an air conditioner and you're going home deaf and numb!

Have you tried to get an air-conditioning service man these days? They're like doctors. They don't make house calls.

Yesterday my wife and I brought our one-ton unit in for diagnosis. Cost us $10 but in all fairness, he did tell us what was wrong with it. It didn't work.

Then he put the air conditioner and our savings account on the critical list.

But we do have a lot to be thankful for. It'll only cost us $83 with delivery guaranteed—for the first cool day in October.

AIRLINES

The 2,000-mile-an-hour airliner project has been canceled. Someone just realized, at three times the speed of sound, who could hear the movies?

It's amazing how important movies have become to flying. Yesterday they grounded a plane because of a bad projector.

And problems! Yesterday I'm flying in from California and I get up to go to the washroom. Little do I know it's a picture where they don't seat you after the first ten minutes. . . . Fortunately, there was a seat where I was.

I've only one complaint about these in-flight movies. If it's a lousy picture, just try to get your $150 back!

I don't wanna mention any names, but I flew on one airline that's so cheap, they don't show movies—slides!

I took one of those economy airlines that save you money 'cause they're slower. This one was really economical. Got there two hours after the boat!

Did you hear about the airline whose planes were always showing up twenty to thirty minutes late? And they finally figured out what it was. Tired gasoline!

It's hard to believe, but these new supersonic jets will be able to stop on a dime—providing it's placed at the end of a 10-mile runway. . . . One of them needs so much space to land, they just ruled out Rhode Island.

Personally, I never go economy class. Did you know if you fly this way and there's an accident, you have to stand up in the life raft?

AIR POLLUTION

I got an idea that could save billions of dollars. Instead of putting antismog devices on the cars—why don't they just put Murine in the gas?

Now they've got an air-pollution device for motorcycles. It fits right over the driver.

(YOUR TOWN) has much to be proud of. Beautiful women with the skin you love to touch. Beautiful scenery with the air you're afraid to touch.

Where else, if you want to look at a sewer, do you lean back?

If the smog gets any worse, I got a great idea for a business—Hertz Rent-A-Lung!

This is gonna be the first generation in history ever to breathe factory-second air.

Now there's a group that's demonstrating against air pollution. They sit in front of chimneys and sing: "We Shall Be Overcome."

For people who don't know what smog is—it's a combination of smoke, fog, and legislative inaction.

If the smog doesn't make you cry, the way the authorities are handling it will!

I won't say it's a wishy-washy approach, but if these politicians had been responsible for the Ten Commandments—they would have read: "Thou shalt not (unless you feel strongly to the contrary)."

ALASKA

MARCH 30TH: Today marks the —— anniversary of the purchase of Alaska from Russia and we'd like to bring you the historic words spoken on that occasion: (COUNTING) "$6,900,000. $7,000,000. $7,100,000. $7,200,000. There you are—paid in full!" (RUSSIAN ACCENT) "Comrade!" "Yes?" "No Green Stamps?"

You remember Alaska. The biggest snow job the country ever got till the last election.

Instead of competing, I think Alaska and Texas ought to cooperate. For instance, Alaska could be a paradise if the air was just a little warmer. And who has more hot air than Texas?

ANXIETY

Today we're experiencing anxieties people never even dreamed of twenty years ago. Like the feeling of guilt that comes over you when you write out a check to the *Reader's Digest* with a ball-point you got from *Look!*

Everybody's feeling guilty about something. I just saw a three-layer, chocolate-marshmallow birthday cake—but it comes with saccharine candles!

People are so emotional these days. Yesterday I saw someone voting "DON'T KNOW" with a clenched fist.

Jittery? I wanna tell you how nervous people are. The newest calorie books give the count for fingernails.

I wouldn't say I'm nervous. It's just that the butterflies in my stomach are like the Strategic Air Command. Some of them flying at all times.

I'm not feeling myself today. I think I only got 60 per cent of my Minimum Daily Requirement of Riboflavin.

I'm as nervous as a tree on the *Lassie* show.

I'm so nervous, I can't even eat. What's the right wine to go with fingernails?

A neurotic is a person who's still worried he might have looked at that last eclipse too much.

Adjustment is watching that old movie *Remember Pearl Harbor* on a Sony.

ARMY

I think the Pentagon is so wrong in not drafting married men. These are the only recruits the Army gets who really know how to take orders.

You can tell the Army is taking them younger. One of the new outfits is called the 485th Skateboard Battalion!

The Government is gonna draft fifteen hundred young doctors. I don't know if it's for the Army or they're stocking a cruise ship!

People wanna know why the Army needs fifteen hundred doctors with practices. Simple. It's cheaper than two million mothers with chicken soup!

All army doctors are first lieutenants or better—except one who's a private first class. Ever since he gave that general a thermometer and told him what to do with it.

When I was in the Army we used to play medical roulette. We had six doctors and one of them was an obstetrician. . . . And he couldn't forget the old routine. He had two chairs—no waiting.

Have you ever seen those obstetrical chairs? You look like a naked astronaut! . . . And I'm strapped naked in one chair and another guy's strapped naked in the other. I said: "Isn't this ridiculous? All I've got is a sore throat!" He said: "What are you complaining about? I'm delivering a telegram!"

One time I went to an Army doctor and I said: "Doc, you gotta do something. I've got this terrible headache!" He said: "Headache? You're putting me on. You mean to say if you were a civilian, you'd come to me about a headache?" I said: "Doc, if I were a civilian, I wouldn't come to you. I'd send for you!"

The enemy claims we're using poison gas in Vietnam, which is ridiculous. But I think I know what happened. Somehow, the exhaust from an army kitchen must have blown their way.

You see, army cooking was never meant for Orientals. I'll take that one step further. Army cooking was never meant for human beings!

We used to get food so tough, even the corn flakes had to be marinated!

Did you hear about the call girl who was arrested outside of the Pentagon—for contributing to the delinquency of a major?

ART

I've always envied those Indian statues with the six hands. Ever since I had poison ivy.

I like that picture of Whistler's mother 'cause it really tells a story. Here's this old lady—waiting for the TV set to come back from the repair shop.

I was reading the story of Michelangelo, the Italian painter who spent seven years painting the ceiling of the Sistine Chapel. Five years finding the numbers and two years filling them in.

Just think! Seven years to get a ceiling painted. They must have the same landlord I do!

And after seven years up on this scaffold, painting, painting, painting—he finally calls down and says: "What do you think?" And a voice calls back: "I said 'blue'!"

All this happened four hundred years ago and I'm glad. Can you imagine if they asked an artist today to paint the ceiling of the Sistine Chapel? How would it look up there—a can of tomato soup?

Then there's the *Mona Lisa*. The picture that looks like your wife does when you say you had to work late at the office.

Do you realize the *Mona Lisa* is 456 years old? The *Mona Lisa* was done by Michelangelo, who specialized in religious pictures. Sort of a sixteenth-century Charlton Heston.

In a way, it's amazing the popularity this picture has. Through the years, tens of millions of people have gone out of their way to see this girl—who, in real life, couldn't make it in an Over 28 club.

A lot of people are fascinated by the sly, questioning smile. Not me. I see it every year on the face of my tax examiner.

It's no wonder the *Mona Lisa* is so popular with Americans. It's the only thing in France that smiles at us!

ASTRONAUTS

Nowadays the all-American boy doesn't dare drink milk, exercise, or eat spinach. Doesn't want to get too big to fit into the capsule.

There's been a lot of speculation about sending up a woman astronaut. I happen to know that on our next shot, we'll be halfway to making it. We're sending up a fella who lisps.

What a thrill it must be. To be up there so high, there's nothing but you, taxes, and the national debt!

Can you imagine going through spring, summer, autumn, and winter—all in one hour? It's like taking a vacation in Florida.

It's easy to tell when an astronaut is over the hill. He asks for a slower capsule.

ATOMIC ENERGY

You've heard of BAN THE BOMB? What about that other group that wants us to use it? BANG THE BOMB!

Maybe we oughta start calling them Adam bombs, 'cause if we ever start using them, that's what we'll all be back to.

Take my word for it—the British and American governments will never ban the bomb. They couldn't take the risk of five million students with nothing to do after classes.

You know what's wrong with living in a world that exists on the brink of atomic destruction? When you give up that hour in April—you're never sure you're gonna get it back again in the fall.

I love the way they keep stressing a low-yield atomic bomb. That's the military version of being a little bit pregnant.

20

Frankly, I don't know what a low-yield bomb is. Sounds a little like my wife.

This isn't too widely known, but the Congo has been working on its own version of the H-bomb. It's a blow dart you dip in uranium.

Nuclear submarines have to face three major problems—enemy action, atomic radiation, and the mating season for whales!

B

BABY-SITTERS

We used to have a baby-sitter called Mary Poopins. Everything was too much for her.

We finally figured out a way to make sure she watched the baby. We kept it in the refrigerator!

All this costs you 75¢ an hour. They're not really baby-sitters—they're discount Jesse Jameses!

BASEBALL

I know a ten-year-old who's been watching baseball on TV all summer. He doesn't know much about the game but he shaves magnificently!

Have you seen the Astrodome? There are dozens and dozens of exits all around the building. I asked the architect: "How come there are so many exits?" He said: "Podner, you ever hear of the Alamo?"

Dallas is so envious, it's putting up a building 20,000 feet high. It's for sky diving on rainy days.

You've gotta admit the Astrodome is vast—and into it they've put this half-vast team.

It must be wonderful to live in Houston; go out to the ball park and spend an afternoon in the fresh air conditioning.

I just love the Expos. The only team in America doing reruns of last year's games—live!

It's really unnecessary to say the Expos are in the cellar. They've been in the cellar so long, they're growing mushrooms in their spare time.

Frankly, I never believed in euthanasia until the Expos.

I got a great idea. Why don't we hold a World Drearies in October? Between the (N.L. CELLAR TEAM) and the (A.L. CELLAR TEAM)?

Americans are people who wonder why other countries resent us—but who see nothing wrong with calling it the World Series.

BIRTH CONTROL

My wife happens to be an expert on family planning. The day after we got married, half her family moved in with us—and the other half was planning to.

They're always talking about birth-control devices. My wife uses the oldest birth-control device in the world. Pretends she's asleep.

But it's amazing how strong the feeling for birth control is in this country. Why, you can't drive two miles without seeing a sign saying: WATCH OUT FOR CHILDREN!

In India housewives can now dial for birth-control information. All they have to remember is two letters—N O!

Do you realize what this means—dialing for birth-control information? Twenty years from now there are gonna be people on this earth who owe their existence to a wrong number!

Science is really amazing. Now they're combining that new fertility drug with a birth-control pill. It's for people who don't want triplets.

I don't know why they keep talking about birth control like it was something new. We had the same thing twenty-five years ago only it was called Army Coffee.

24

I'm a little suspicious of some of these birth-control pills. Like, one of the leading side effects seems to be pregnancy.

Now they've got a new birth-control pill. You take it and for twenty-four hours you go: (SHAKE HEAD FROM SIDE TO SIDE).

Another birth-control pill is made of celery, peanut butter, and taffy. By the time you get finished chewing, you're too tired!

They say that because of the oral birth-control pills, women in their sixties and seventies might still have babies. They do now—their daughters'!

One store is adding a whole new line of maternity shawls.

"Grandma, what big eyes you've got! Grandma, what big ears you've got! Grandma, what a big—oh no, not again?"

Frankly, I think it's gonna be a little embarrassing, a seventy-year-old woman giving birth—especially to a forty-year-old baby!

And it will be a challenge to their husbands. I know some of these old codgers are heir-minded. Now let's see if they're heir-conditioned!

Have you heard about the latest birth-control device? It's a pair of slacks and the legs aren't permanently creased—they're permanently crossed.

Personally, I think all these birth-control pills are ridiculous. You need the control a lot earlier than that!

But everything is getting so complicated these days. Remember when we were teen-agers? Birth control wasn't a pill. It was narrow cars!

And the birth rate would be a lot lower than it is if it wasn't for three things: early marriages, drive-in movies, and high schools.

BUSINESS

I just found out why more executives don't make passes at their secretaries. It's the wife backlash!

My wife has been very suspicious of my new secretary ever since she found out her name—Carmen Sutra!

There's so much polite bribery going on—especially with liquor. People who have never heard of the Bill of Rights—still wanna take the Fifth!

They claim gangsters have taken over and are actually running some banks. Well, I was talking to our local bank president and I said: "It's ridiculous—gangsters taking over banks. That could never happen here—could it, Little Louie?"

I don't know if crooks are running the bank, but the last three holdups were by cops!

And you've never seen such mean-looking tellers—which makes for some problems. Yesterday I went in and said: "I want to take out $2,000." He said: "How much?" I said: "I want to take out $500." He said: "How much?" I said: "$50?" He said: "How much?" I said: "Here's ten bucks. I'll mail in the rest!"

And when they lend you money, they've got a wonderful system to make sure you bring it back again. You don't leave.

They've got this vault in the basement with containers 6 feet long. They're called Safe Depositor Boxes.

The only way you can tell when they take over a bank is by little things. Like your account is still insured for $10,000—but you gotta go to Sicily to get it.

C

CALIFORNIA

I know the pioneers had a rough time of it going west to California. No Howard Johnsons. No sunglasses. No A.A.A. But at least they didn't have to worry about someone pulling out to pass them on hills!

I don't care what you say about nuclear bombs, missiles, germ warfare—California still has the greatest deterrent of them all. Community Property!

They say brevity is the soul of wit. In California, it's the front of waitresses!

They've got some swingin' groups out there in California. I saw one with the motto: PRAY TO KEEP PRAYERS OUT OF SCHOOLS!

CARS

I'm fascinated by the new cars. They're sort of a compromise. Last year's styling with next year's prices.

You know what puzzles me about cars? What do you do with a fastback in winter? Let's face it—that isn't just a window back there. It's a glove compartment for snow!

Have you noticed how much bigger cars are getting? I noticed it yesterday when I saw that sports car. The one with the walk-in glove compartment.

But a car is a very dangerous place. Ask any girl who's ever parked in one!

I had a terrible experience this morning. Really. My Jaguar ate up my Mustang.

My wife's had a Mustang for two weeks and she's worried sick. Where do you put the oats?

A Cadillac is what a doctor buys to not make house calls in.

CAR ACCESSORIES

There's one new car on the market that has more than sixty optional extras. What makes this so unusual—the motor is one of them.

Sixty optional extras! Remember the good old days—when a car was put together by Detroit instead of you?

You know what's fun, though? Combining the extras! Like, have you ever considered a power glove compartment? . . . Everything falls out electronically.

I know a fella who had a phone put in his Edsel and all he can get is calls from Packards.

Boy, those used-car dealers are so sneaky. I once bought a car and they said it had factory air. And it did—smoke, dust, fumes!

Thanks to air conditioning, couples in the back seat have a new worry—pneumonia!

CAR SAFETY DEVICES

What a great idea! Factory-second seat belts for people who wanna be half safe!

Have you heard about the latest safety device? It's a steering column in the form of a stake. It only goes through your heart if you're a vampire!

Do you realize, what with front seat belts and foldaway steering wheels—a girl today doesn't stand a chance?

CHILDREN

Once the civil rights problem is settled, then let's all get together and work for the betterment of the most oppressed, downtrodden, and harassed minority of them all—parents!

I've got nothing against children, but if my wife starts talking about the patter of little feet around the house—she better mean mice!

Personally, I believe kids should be seen and not heard. And the way they look today, I'm not even sure about that.

You know what's a big ploy with kids today? They look at you and say: "Did I ask to be born?" I always say: "If you had, the answer would have been NO!"

Quintuplets: I understand that couple are calling them quintups —cause they're afraid to say "Let's" again.

I don't know how she feels about it but after she gave him quintuplets—she also gave him another surprise. His own bedroom!

They say quintuplets happen just once every fifty-four million times. What I wanna know is: How did she ever find time to do her housework?

The doctor said there was nothing unusual about the delivery. He just had to keep sending out for wider forceps.

Parents have such romantic ideas—like how they're going to tell their kids about the facts of life. It'll be the first day of spring. The mother robins will be hatching their eggs. The salmon will be fighting their way upstream. Bees will be fertilizing the little buttercups. Their kids will look up in wonderment at this eternal drama of life ever renewing itself—and *that* will be the time! You know how it actually works out? Yesterday we were in a hardware store and my kid says: "What's a female plug?"

Kids do get confused. I know a six-year-old who came home from her first day in Sunday school and she was telling her

29

parents all about the group singing. They asked her: "What did they sing?" She said: "I don't know what they sang, but I sang '(CURRENT TV SINGING COMMERCIAL)'!"

As far as I'm concerned, Walter Keane is 100 per cent right. Most kids' eyes are bigger than their stomachs.

CHRISTMAS

CHRISTMAS—the time when kids and money both sprout wings.

Have you noticed how many new charities there are this year? The Society for the Rehabilitation of Las Vegas Losers. . . . The American Nudist Foundation—"Let's Put the Eve Back in New Year's!". . . . And the John Brunch Society for late eaters!

Do you realize that Charles Dickens' immortal A *Christmas Carol* would be impossible today? Tiny Tim would be covered by Major Medical. . . . Jacob Marley would be in Forest Lawn— and who'd want to leave that? . . . And Scrooge. Scrooge would be a candidate for the Conservatives.

And in this day and age, you just don't go around saying: "God bless us, every one!" Right away, someone would want to know: "Does that mean the Communists too?"

I don't want to brag, but I'm gonna make a fortune this Christmas. I just cornered the frankincense and myrrh market!

Frankincense and myrrh. Do you realize that last year alone, these two words sold four thousand dictionaries?

Isn't this a wonderful time of the year? When all over the world Christmas candles are burning. (PEER INTO THE DISTANCE.) Oh, I'm sorry. Those are United States embassies.

December 25th is the day churches all over the country are jampacked with Easter-Christmas Christians. People who go to their church twice a year and their Chrismas Club fifty times a year —which kinda says what they worship the most.

But things seem to happen this time of the year. December is the month when the Christmas Club you didn't join in January, sends you an empty envelope!

For those of you who have never joined a Christmas Club—it's a well-thought-out plan to keep you poor from January through November—so the stores can be rich in December.

We had the wildest Christmas dinner ever. We let the kids cook it. You know how after a Christmas dinner you usually take bicarbonate to settle it? This is the first time we ever had to take Tums to settle the bicarbonate!

I love those Christmas fruitcakes. You sink your choppers into them and you don't know if you're eating or a test pilot for Polident!

I wanna tell you what kind of luck I've got. If this year I cornered the mistletoe market—they'd postpone Christmas!

CHRISTMAS DAY: I want to wish you all a very Merry Christmas. And for those of you who don't observe Christmas—a very Happy Chanukah! And for those of you who don't observe Chanukah either—how come you ain't at work today?

CHRISTMAS CARDS

Are you finished with your Christmas cards? You know, I think I finally figured out why the Frankenstein monster goes around with his hands like this: (CLUTCHING CLAWS). From addressing three hundred Christmas cards!

Personally, I've licked so many flaps, I even burp sticky!

I like to get them done early but in show business you can't really send out Christmas cards on December 1st. There's no way of telling who your friends are gonna be three weeks later.

Insecurity is getting depressed if you send out more Christmas cards than you receive.

You can always tell the secure people in this world. They're the ones who send their boss the same-price Christmas card they send the rest of the list.

I had a terrible experience with the outfit that printed my Christmas cards. Ran the whole front cover backwards. Two hundred people I wished: LEON! LEON!

And every Christmas you run into those tricky gift cards—like: "5,000 GREEN STAMPS HAVE BEEN DONATED IN YOUR NAME TO S & H!"

CHRISTMAS—when you exchange hellos with strangers and good buys with friends.

You'd be amazed how farsighted people are. Nothing increases the amount of Christmas cards you get in December—like planning to build a swimming pool in July.

They say the average family sends out 75 Christmas cards—50 before Christmas and 25 before New Year's to people you've forgotten.

If the Post Office really had the Christmas spirit, they'd postmark every Christmas card mailed up to Lincoln's Birthday—December 24th.

This year the Post Office is going a little further with those special Christmas stamps. The glue will be flavored eggnog.

I'm a little confused. I got my first Christmas card today. And the way the mails are, I'm not even sure it's this year's.

The only Christmas cards I can't take are the ones who show up at office parties.

My wife and I have a working agreement when it comes to Christmas. She signs the cards and I sign the checks.

CHRISTMAS DECORATIONS

Christmas is the time when people put so many bulbs on the outside of their houses, you don't know if they're celebrating the birth of Jesus or General Electric.

Christmas is a special time of the year for me. Every December 15th, I get out a string of fifteen hundred colored lights, climb up to the roof, and spell out: BAH! HUMBUG!

Do you know what it is to put up fifteen hundred Christmas lights on the roof of a house? The kids are giving two to one I'm gonna come down the chimney before Santa Claus does!

1500 lights! Every time I shut it off, the electric company says: (STARTLED) "What was that?"

I'm also big for mistletoe. Last year I hung mistletoe over our front door and said: "The next person who comes through that door—wow!" Did you ever taste a mailman?

You know what shakes me? Did you know that most of the mistletoe you see around these days is plastic? I didn't until this morning—when I stood under a sprig and had an uncontrollable desire to kiss a transistor radio!

My wife bought an aluminum Christmas tree this year—and looking at it standing there in the corner, it brought a plastic tear to my eye.

I don't wanna complain about my wife, but you're looking at the only fella in town who doesn't have to deck the halls with boughs of holly. It's still there from last year.

You see all the new look Christmas trees? Red, gold, silver? Ours is gray—dust!

CHRISTMAS MUSIC

My neighbor has his sound system playing the "Silent Night Bossa Nova" over twenty-six amplifiers. Yesterday I phoned him and said: "Do you know it's three o'clock on Christmas morning?" He said: "No, but find out the label and I'll get it!"

This year there's gonna be realism in Christmas. The hit song'll be: "I Saw Mommy Nagging Santa Claus."

Wouldn't it be awful if forty years ago, all Terry-Thomas wanted for Christmas was his two front teeth—and these are the ones he got?

My wife happens to be very opposed to one of those Christmas songs: "You better not pout, you better not shout." Two of her best weapons!

So this Salvation Army band plays its last "Silent Night," trudges back to the mission and hands in the money. The major counts it: "Only $6.42?" The leader answers: "Man, with these arrangements, you're lucky we got that!"

Christmas in Los Angeles is always interesting. Seeing carolers dressed in Bermuda shorts . . . groping their way through the smog singing: "It came upon a midnight clear."

And farther South, in Mexico, they have their own versions of carols: "Deck the Halls with Hot Tamales"!

I love that carol "What Child Is This?" Sounds like parents sorting kids after a Christmas party.

I love to sing those wonderful old carols like "Oh Little Town of Bethlehem." I just figured out what kept Bethlehem a little town. Maybe (POLITICAL FIGURE) was mayor.

Did you hear about the little kid who's supposed to sing in a Sunday school Christmas service and his parents ask him what hymn he's going to sing. He says: "That hymn about the King nobody likes." They're completely confused: "The hymn about the King nobody likes? Who's that?" He says: "Good King Wences—the Louse!"

I don't know whether they should make such a big thing of Christmas in schools—'cause not all the kids believe in it. Like, in my apartment building, there's a little Jewish kid named Saul. And they picked him to be in a Christmas chorus. The kid went through all kinds of mental battles with his conscience, his beliefs, his background. Fortunately, he settled it by singing the traditional hymns but with his own lyrics. Like: " 'Tis the season; call me Solly . . . Good King Wendelbaum . . . and the ever-popular: 'O Little Town of Tel Aviv.' "

CHRISTMAS PAGEANTS

Every Christmas pageant throughout the world has a scene showing Joseph leading Mary into Bethlehem on a donkey. Do you realize what would happen if the Republicans asked for equal time?

You know what's fascinating? A Sunday school pageant in Beverly Hills—where all the rich kids are. You'd have to see it to believe it. Two kids were dressed up as Mary and Joseph and they're on their way to the inn in Bethlehem. And here's where you could tell it was Beverly Hills. On the opposite side of the stage there's this other kid dressed in a shepherd's outfit—and he's wiring ahead for reservations!

So these three wise men are following a star in the East and two of them are staring at the third: "Myrrh? This is what you call a Christmas present?"

Have you noticed that most kids today don't really know what a crèche is? They think it's a carport for people.

CHRISTMAS PARTIES

How come, every time you throw a party, there's thousands of dollars' worth of chairs and sofas—and everybody sits on the floor? . . . I know an outfit that's making a fortune selling bucket-seat rugs!

Christmas is also the time for office parties. I won't say how husbands carry on at office parties—but yesterday someone sang "O Come, All Ye Faithful"—and only two showed up!

Sometimes I wonder if office parties are planned so much for fun as revenge. . . . They all seem to follow a pattern. Sandwiches and bosses both get cut up into little pieces.

Canapés are always a big thing at office parties. For those of you not familiar with *canapés,* they're a piece of corrugated cut into a hundred little shapes—and smeared with library paste and pimento. . . . Then on others is a blob of—well, it's kinda hard to describe. Picture BBs mixed with axle grease . . . I wouldn't dare call it caviar 'cause the Russians are mad enough at us as it is.

And there's never enough ice cubes. Here we are the richest nation on earth, and at every office party we have to ration water.

But the boss always goes the whole route. Orders a medley of forty-five sandwiches—six of which get eaten. . . . But they never go to waste 'cause at the end of the party, everybody has a dog who loves delicatessen.

You know one thing common to all office parties? Paper cups! And there is one thing common to all paper cups—they leak. . . . I've spilled so much liquor on my tie—they don't dry-clean it any more. They distill it.

Then there's the office-party carol: "Check the Halls for Saul and Mollie."

I don't know why people knock office parties. Anything that lets you eat, drink, and dissipate on company time can't be all bad.

Office parties wouldn't be so bad if it wasn't for the sixty-minute affairs. Really! It's amazing the way people who never even look at each other the rest of the year suddenly get hot under the white collar. . . . And secretaries learn they can lose a lot more than letters behind those files!

But even office parties are changing. I went to one where a computer spent two hours telling me about its operation.

I just heard a wild story. They held a Christmas party in a completely automated office. And the computer got drunk and tried to unfasten the electric typewriter's ribbon!

36

But people just seem to bust loose at office parties. They do things they'd never think of doing the rest of the year—like busting into the bookkeeping department and bending and folding IBM cards.

I think it's fine to have a little horseplay, but sending bankruptcy notices to your five biggest accounts!

The person you have to watch out for at office parties is the eager beaver who doesn't drink. Sips ginger ale; calls it a highball; then stands around watching—and remembering. . . . If this is your assistant, fire him in the morning. Remember what happened to Trotsky!

CHRISTMAS PRESENTS

If you really wanna have an exciting holiday—make an agreement with your wife that you won't exchange gifts for Christmas. Then don't.

If you really wanna get even with somebody who's always talking about an old-fashioned Christmas—send them a partridge in a pear tree.

I once sent someone a partridge in a pear tree and it was just wonderful what I got back in return. A summons from the A.S.P.C.A.

I know a fella who gives sadistic Christmas presents—like a down payment on a Rolls-Royce.

Hey, if you know any hypochondriacs, I got a great Christmas present for them. It costs $300 and comes in chests—pneumonia!

I just bought the perfect Christmas present for my mother-in-law. A leaky ant farm!

How's this for an appalling Christmas present? A pool table to people who live in a trailer.

I just wanna know one thing. Where do people in trailers hide Christmas presents?

This Christmas, if you really wanna give a gift that keeps on giving—how about a pregnant cat?

I know a couple that are having an international Christmas. He's getting an English smoking jacket—and she's getting a Mexican divorce.

My wife has a little Christmas present problem with me this year. It's: What to give a man who has everything—up to here!

She hasn't spoken to me since Labor Day, and I figure—the least I can do is buy her a little Christmas present to show my appreciation.

My wife gets kinda sentimental around Christmas time. She always likes to get something I created myself. Last year I gave her an ulcer.

I want to get my wife one of those sports cars with bucket seats for Christmas—now if I can only find one with a bucket big enough.

But I saved my wife a lot of standing in line this Christmas. I didn't give her a present—I gave her an exchange certificate. Who needs a middleman?

My kids love to get me useful, practical, down-to-earth-type gifts. Last year they gave me a battery-operated toothpick.

Sometimes I get the feeling that if there were no such thing as Christmas, Father's Day, and Dad's birthday—after-shave lotion wouldn't exist!

You know what I'd like to give to the girl who has everything? Me!

This Christmas, why not give your minister the very best? Stained-glass contact lenses!

I know it's the thought and not the gift that counts—but couldn't people think a little bigger?

You've heard of the lay-away plan? I always buy Christmas presents on the lie-away plan. When they ask me how I'm gonna pay for it, I just lie away!

CHRISTMAS—SANTA CLAUS

Christmas—the time when everybody gets a little Santamental.

It's interesting how many people who don't believe in Santa Claus will go out and buy sweepstakes tickets.

Isn't that awful? Assigning Santa Claus a Zip Code number? "Ho, ho, ho, ho. This is 99701 talking. Call me Nine, Nine for short!" Nine-nine. Sounds like a Bavarian virgin.

It doesn't make sense—like a green Santa Claus outfit.

Jackie Gleason has a wonderful time around Christmas. He's the only one I know who needs a stretch Santa Claus outfit.

You know what's an eerie experience? Christmas in California! To see a department-store Santa Claus—and right above the whiskers, he's peeling.

Santa Claus is my idea of a well-adjusted individual. Can you imagine driving through all this weather—and still being able to say "Ho, ho, ho"?

I don't wanna say anything about Rudolph and his red nose, but I understand A.A. just put him on their most-wanted list.

Incidentally, Santa Claus won't be making the rounds this year. He's still down at the Internal Revenue Service trying to explain the six billion dollars he put down for gifts last year.

The Russians have been so quiet, I'm afraid they're up to no good somewhere. Wouldn't it be awful if they were feeding Metrecal to Santa Claus?

Christmas is when you see hundreds of Santa Clauses all over town. Two women were standing outside this department store and a big, fat Santa Claus went in one side of the revolving door—and a skinny little Santa Claus came out the other. One woman nudged the other and said: "Sarah, that's what I call a diet!"

I'm a little worried about the boys on our local basketball team. Especially their coordination. One of them just flunked Santa Claus. Couldn't shake the bell and say "Ho! Ho! Ho!" at the same time!

Did you hear about the kid in Peyton Place who saw Mommy kissing Santa Claus, and the butler, and the gardener, and the milkman, and the—?

Kids are so shrewd today. They go up to the department store Santa Claus and tell him everything they want for Christmas—but in a voice loud enough for Grandma to hear.

Sometimes I get the feeling the Santa Claus story is dying a little each year. You tell it to a seven-year-old today and right away he wants to know how many pounds of thrust the sleigh develops before it leaves the launching pad. . . . You start with Dancer and Prancer after that.

CHRISTMAS SHOPPING

Christmas brings about such wonderful feelings of warmth and good will. Like yesterday I was in a department store and heard a wife say to her husband: "Let's get him one of those animals you pull along that quacks and clatters and rings and bumps. That's what they did to us last year."

You know what's a frightening experience? Taking your family of six kids through a toy department. It's like playing Russian roulette with your bank balance.

You hear such fascinating conversations in the department stores. Like a father trying to explain to his three-year-old that a reindeer isn't a horse with TV antenna.

Have you noticed when going Christmas shopping, when you don't know what you're looking for—you usually find it much faster than when you do?

And one Golden Rule for Christmas shopping—Bring Money! Nowadays, the only thing you can get without money, is depressed.

I know a woman who bought $2,000 worth of Christmas presents and the next day got her money back. Then she bought $4,000 worth of Christmas presents and the next day she got her money back. Then she bought $6,000 worth and the next day she got her money back. I said: "What's the point?" She said: "The Green Stamps you keep!"

Christmas is getting so commercial, the way things are going, I don't know whether we're celebrating the birth of Jesus or Easy Payments.

I think one radio announcer really said it. He gave a sixty-second pitch for a $19.95 toy. Then introduced that meaningful hymn: "It Came upon a Midnight Dear."

Incidentally, I got an idea that could save millions of dollars for parents all over the country. Why don't we let Barbie go nudist?

Every year, Christmas becomes less a birthday and more a Clearance Sale.

Personally, I didn't really believe they had overcommercialized Christmas until I saw that duplex crèche.

Have you been in the stores yet? It's unbelievable. You don't walk—you just get carried along with the crowd. I turned to one woman and said: "Have you ever seen such confusion?" She said: "You oughta know. This is the ladies' room!"

But I just love going into the stores saying: "Ho! Ho! Ho!" Then seeing the prices: "Oh! Oh! Oh!"

A salesgirl's version of that famous poem: "'Twas the nightmare before Christmas—"

One Christmas perennial is the story of the last-minute, hectic, noise-filled, desperate rush for gifts at a downtown department store. A salesgirl was jotting down a customer's name and address when she paused, looked up at the milling throng, and ventured: "It's a madhouse, isn't it?" Came the answer: "No, it's a private home."

Yes, when it comes to department stores, Christmas is the greatest thing to happen to inventories since matches.

Really—come December 24th, they can sell anything. Consider. On July 6th, would you ever think of buying your husband embroidered jockey shorts? . . . That's what I got last year—embroidered jockey shorts. Feels like you're sitting on two pages of braille. . . . Thanks to embroidered jockey shorts, at this very moment, my scratching is six months ahead of my itching!

But thanks to right thinking, Christmas is in my heart twelve months a year. And thanks to time payments, it's in my checkbook likewise.

POST-CHRISTMAS LINES: You know, with all these sales going on, you could save a fortune just by celebrating Christmas on January 5th?

Doesn't it grab you to see something you paid $80 for, going for $49.50—and now they'll deliver?

Anyone interested in a good buy on some used Christmas wrapping paper?

CHRISTMAS TIPPING

What I give my building superintendent for Christmas makes him remember me the whole year through—nothing!

You may think of it as Christmas, but to elevator operators it's more like CROSS THE PALM SUNDAY.

Everybody's getting so cynical about Christmas. In fact, the only people today who still believe in Santa Claus are elevator operators, doormen, and janitors!

I have a feeling Christmas is near. The building superintendent just came up and offered to fix my air conditioner.

Some buildings give you a Christmas list of all the elevator operators, the janitor, the porters. They put all their begs in one ask-it!

Believe me, Christmas is the only time I ever see some of these people clean up!

I just got my first Christmas card from the superintendent of the building. I didn't mind that so much. It was the business-reply envelope in it.

This man is so sure he deserves a present—two more Christmases and he's gonna think it's *his* birthday!

I also got an awfully sweet card from the garage attendants:
Christmas time is almost here,
Giving you a choice that's clear;
Send a check or legal tender,
Or find yourself a fender mender!

And elevator operators get very solicitous too. Like during the entire month of December, if you don't want to, you don't have to face the front of the car.

Do you realize, if it wasn't for Christmas, most people would never know an elevator can be stopped on a level with the floor?

It's amazing how many elevator operators have showed up to wish me a Merry Christmas. Four and it's only December 5th! What makes it even more amazing, I live in a walk-up!

And isn't it fantastic the way elevator operators can say "Merry Christmas!" in the very same sneer they say "Good morning" in the rest of the year?

I mean, it isn't as if you're asking them a favor—like going crosstown, or something like that. . . . All you wanna do is go up and down—preferably in that order.

You know what's always bugged me about elevator operators? The ones who say: "Watch your step!" I mean, I get enough of that from my wife!

43

CHRISTMAS TOYS

Christmas morning—when a child goes into each present tense.

Christmas is such an exciting time—playing with all the toys you've given yourself via the kids.

I can't help it. I'm one of those fathers—nothing is too good for my kids. Like for Christmas I gave them a toy fire engine—complete with three fires.

But I made one terrible mistake. I also got them one of those indestructible toys—and it is. Now when they leave it in the driveway, it's my car that breaks.

Christmas morning is always a traumatic experience. Seeing your daughter try to trade her brand-new bicycle for the kid next door's coloring book.

If you really wanna get even with that noisy kid next door, give him a Christmas present. A brand-new electric train with forty feet of track—all of it straight!

Some of these manufacturers are so sneaky. I know one who sells a toy microscope for $11.98—but the germs are extra.

It's fascinating the new toys they've got for Christmas. One is called a Neurotic Doll. It's wound up already.

Have you seen the dolls they're making for little girls? I have never seen such sexy dolls in my life. One of them comes complete with a bottle—gin!

It's unbelievable. Last year I wanted to buy a wedding gown for one of these dolls—$5.98. $5.98! I didn't buy it. Let her sneak off to motels!

Remember the good old days—when a doll was a pink, chubby, shapeless lump? . . . Remember? I married one!

Kids really love these talking dolls 'cause they say the same few things over and over again. I think they're modeled after my mother-in-law.

One day I went shopping for a doll and it was fascinating. The clerk said: "How about this one? It drinks and it wets and it cries." I said: "I'm not surprised!"

All the toys this Christmas are electronic—robots, rockets, walkie-talkies, space stations. For those of you who wanna give the ideal after-Christmas gift—two dozen batteries.

Have you noticed how all the new toys need batteries? Years ago, your biggest problem on a cold Christmas morning was getting the car started. Now it's getting the toys started.

Remember the good old days, when the power needed to operate toys came from kids instead of batteries?

Now almost every toy requires some kind of battery. Hell today, for a modern American mother, is a rainy day with three kids and dead batteries!

And because of batteries, kids don't play with toys any more. They observe them! . . . They watch them do all the things they would be doing if they didn't have the toys in the first place.

You think I'm kidding, but the first outfit that puts out a battery-operated football that throws itself is gonna make a fortune!

Thanks to batteries, you never have to worry about a kid getting a broken leg, or a fractured wrist, or a bruised knee any more. Electrocuted, yes!

"D" batteries—that's the magic word. I still don't know if that's the manufacturer's description or a parent's abbreviation.

You buy them by the dozen 'cause this is one present that really keeps on giving——out!

You know another frightening thing? How big the toys are getting. Two feet high, three feet high, four feet high! I mean, it's all right for a kid to have a sibling rivalry—but with a robot?

45

. . . Throws a tantrum every time *it* gets batteries and *he* doesn't! . . .

Naturally, everything's educational. Take these road racing games. It's just wonderful the way they're taking the young, impressionable kids of today—and turning them into the wild-eyed, reckless drivers of tomorrow!

It's all so different from the games we used to play as kids. Remember? The most dangerous thing we could do was sell Boardwalk and Park Place!

I even bought an educational toy. It comes with four square pegs and four round holes. I asked the salesman: "You can't put a square peg in a round hole—so what does it teach?" He said: "Clichés!"

And this year, the big thing is toys that make things. They've got toys that make dresses; toys that make pretzels; toys that make lollipops. They've even got a great big empty box for $19.95. I said: "What does that make?" They said: "$19.95!"

Thanks to lollipop factories, sno-cone syrups, soda-fountain flavors—our entire house is done in a brand-new style. Early Sticky!

One kid was running his lollipop factory and he ran out of raspberry. So he used a bottle from his father's desk. You ever tasted a bourbon lollipop?

Can you ever recall a Christmas when you've seen so many guns and rockets and tanks and missile launchers for kids? It's like they're not making toys for fun any more. For vengeance!

Personally, I don't think we will ever have disarmament. The U.N. may be for it. We may be for it. Russia may be for it. But are the toy manufacturers for it?

Do you realize, if all the model guns and tanks and warplanes were taken out and destroyed—toy departments would look like a supermarket in Cuba?

CHRISTMAS—when you celebrate the birth of the Prince of Peace by giving your kids two rocket launchers, a machine gun, and an atom-bomb kit.

And some of these toy guns are really wild. Like the atom-bomb launcher with the bayonet attached—in case you should miss!

And they've got antitank guns, antiaircraft guns, antibunker guns. They've even got antiauntie guns for kids who don't like their relatives.

I know one kid who had a perfect Christmas. He got eight guns and a victim.

But the real accent is on realistic toys. They've got a gun that really shoots bullets. They've got a bow that really shoots arrows. And they've got a junkie doll that really shoots!

They've got one pistol that's incredible. The kid pulls the trigger and you hear this terrible screaming sound—the neighbors!

Those scale models of nuclear submarines are so realistic, it's frightening. Never mind the Russians infiltrating the Pentagon. Let's just hope they never make it into Macy's!

I saw one toy marked: CHRISTMAS SPECIAL—$15.00! I said: "That's great. What was it before Christmas?" They said: "6.98!"

I just figured out what they mean by unbreakable toys. Those guaranteed to last till New Year's.

CHRISTMAS TREE

FOR JEWISH AUDIENCE: I spent the morning shopping for a Chanukah bush . . . oh, I know which side of the pantry my dishes are buttered on.

I know those artificial Christmas trees are full, uniform, and flameproof—but I've yet to see anybody go up to one, take a deep breath, and say: "Mmmm, smell that plastic!"

47

Personally, I always get a little choked up looking at a vinyl Christmas tree. I realize poems are made by fools like me—but only chemistry can make a tree!

Now they've got vinyl Christmas trees that are so realistic, you can't tell them from the real thing—aluminum!

Vinyl Christmas trees are sort of a tradition in our house. Every year I take the kids out to Dupont and chop one down.

Looking at all these vinyl Christmas trees with the full, balanced branches—the perfectly tapered silhouette—the nonshed needles —I wonder if God ever feels inadequate?

Yesterday I bought my tree and the clerk said: "Do you have any decorative icicles?" I said: "I certainly do. My wife and my secretary!"

Of course, there are a lot of artificial trees on the market—but somehow, those silver, celluloid branches don't make it for me. I mean, it's not like we're celebrating the birth of Dupont.

Discount! That's the magic word these days. I just saw a place selling discount Christmas trees—as if God put a list price on them.

Have you tried to buy a tree yet? The prices! I paid $6 for one and I brought it home in the car. Not the trunk—the glove compartment.

Where do they get all these pygmy Christmas trees? It's like a whole forest went on Metrecal!

I have never seen a tree so weak. I put the star on and it wasn't a tree any more. It was an arch.

I spent a quiet day taking down the Christmas tree. Actually, it was taking down the branches. The needles came down last week.

It's kinda sad to see something so stately, standing there with bare limbs and just a few bits of tinsel clinging to it. That's why I never liked burlesque.

COLOR TELEVISION

Fall is going to be fantastic this year. The whole countryside ablaze with yellows and golds and browns and reds. Not leaves. Color TV!

I think color TV is coming in just in time. I've got a set that's so old, it's gray and white!

Frankly, watching color is nothing new to me. I've got a wife who dyes her hair. . . . She's dyed it so many times, she's the only woman I know with plaid dandruff!

I just bought one of those chiropractic color TV sets. You have to keep making adjustments.

I didn't realize anything was wrong with the color until I found myself saluting the flag of our country—the pink, orange, and blue!

I know a fella who bought a $99 color TV set. Now every Tuesday night he watches Green Skelton.

The nice part about watching color TV—if the good guy calls the bad guy a yellow-belly—you can verify it!

Is it true, on color TV you don't have snow—you have confetti?

Thanks to orange lipstick and green make-up, girls are finally going to look the way they do on color TV.

Did I get a thrill Christmas morning! I thought my wife had given me a six-inch color TV set. But it was a radio with borsch on it!

It's amazing how many people are waiting for them to perfect color TV. I'm still waiting for them to perfect radio.

Would you believe it? Some of these color TV sets sell for $599 and there aren't enough to go 'round? Not the sets—the money!

Color TV is great for people who give up smoking. It gives you something to do with your hands. . . . Believe me, I got this set and in two weeks, I've done more fiddling than Yehudi Menuhin.

And my set has VHF. I asked the salesman: "What does that mean?" He said: "Very High Financing!"

Did you ever feel like singing: "Oh, it costs me a lot, but there's one thing that I've got—color TV, color TV!"

I've been watching TV in color for years. Cheap contact lenses!

Color TV is presenting all kinds of new problems. To be successful, a show doesn't have to be good. It just has to match the drapes!

There's only one trouble with watching TV in glorious color. You turn it off and the world's in black and white!

COMIC STRIPS

Is it true Phyllis Diller's hairdresser used to be Little Orphan Annie's dress designer?

Here's a girl who's forty years old and you oughta see her figure. I think she models for ironing boards!

And she has this dog Sandy—an obedience-school dropout!

Believe me, I'm not putting down Sandy. Why, just yesterday Sandy said: "Arf! Arf!" That's just the way he put it: "Arf! Arf!" Now that may not mean much to you, but to Lassie it's a bon mot!

I just figured out what's wrong with Little Orphan Annie. She's got her contact lenses in sideways!

I'll never forget the time Superman jumped over the Empire State Building. I've had jockey shorts like that myself!

Be honest now. Don't you think Superman is a little unbelievable? I don't mean the jumping over tall buildings; seeing through walls; running faster than express trains. But when have you ever seen a mild-mannered reporter?

COMPUTERS

Did you know that computers come in male and female models? Neither did I until I saw a mechanic walk toward one with an oil can—and the computer was backing away yelling: "Death before dishonor!"

Last year automation gave us eighty-three million additional hours of leisure time—and digital dialing took it away.

I won't say how important my job was, but when they replaced me with a computer—it was secondhand.

The computer won't really be human until it can make a mistake—then blame it on another machine.

CONSERVATION

Smokey the Bear is now nineteen years old and a lot of people are getting worried. In two more years, he'll be old enough to smoke.

They're coming up with all kinds of wild ideas to conserve water —like banning salted peanuts!

If the reservoirs get any lower, we'll be talking about adding water to the fluoridation.

I'll tell you how bad the water shortage is. You know those dolls they sell to kids? The ones with the kidney problem? . . . First time I ever saw one that wet celery tonic! . . .

The water commissioner spent the weekend at the seashore and almost went out of his mind. All day long listening to the ocean— flushing, flushing!

It's amazing how far highway beautification has gone. Someone just attacked Route 66!

CONSERVATIVES

A Conservative is someone who buckles himself in when riding through a car wash.

I hear Detroit is going after the Southern California Conservative market. It's putting out a Fastback Covered Wagon.

A hundred and sixty years ago we had Conservatives. One of them was watching Robert Fulton test his steamboat. The Conservative kept yelling: "It'll never start! It'll never start!" Just then the steamboat pulled away from the shore and plowed majestically up the Hudson River. And the Conservative yelled after it: "It'll never stop! It'll never stop!"

Even back in Biblical days there were Conservatives. Moses commanded the Red Sea to part and it did. One Conservative nudged another and said: "Go buy stock in a ferry company with him around!"

I know a farmer who's making a fortune selling turkeys to Conservatives. They come with two right wings.

A Conservative is a person who goes to Brigitte Bardot movies and reads the titles.

CRIME

I understand even Israel has a gangster problem—the Kosher Nostra!

There's so much violence in this town, if they really like you they give you the key out of the city.

I don't wanna seem like an opportunist, but wouldn't this be a great place to open a discount hospital?

I'll tell you how bad it is. Clark Kent went into a phone booth to change—and never came out! . . . "Me—go out into that? (SHAKE YOUR HEAD) I may have super strength, but I've got super brains too!"

I hear things are getting so rough in this town, the cops are working on the Buddy System. Which means one of them turns to his partner and says: "Let's go up that dark alley and see what's making that noise." And the other one says: "Not me, Buddy!"

When secretaries work late, they won't go home by themselves any more. They wait for their boss to take them. At least then if they get attacked, it could mean a raise!

I know a girl who carries a whistle but even this isn't perfect. Last night she had her purse snatched, and as the thief was running away, she blew this whistle like mad—and within thirty seconds, you know what happened? She got a cab!

For the first time in history, even the churches are locked up. If you wanna go in and pray, you have to go up to the door, knock three times, and say: "Peter sent me!"

D

DANCING

You know what always bugs me about the ballet? No matter how much I pay for seats, I never can hear a word they're saying.

I love that José Greco with all that stomping on the floor. Man, if this fella ever gets the beat, he's gonna be another Ruby Keeler!

She's a very unusual belly dancer. The belly she dances on is yours!

Wouldn't it be funny if the cha-cha-cha was named by a fella who stuttered—and now we'll never know what he had in mind?

I wonder if visions of sugarplums ever have the nerve to dance in Arthur Murray's head?

Whatever happened to the good old days, when you learned how to dance—so you should look graceful?

DAY CAMPS

Tell me, what is there about kids that makes mothers unable to stand them? . . . Do you realize the fastest-growing industry in the United States today is day camps? They're like Eight-Hour Siberias!

Every morning you can see the kids standing in front of their houses waiting for the bus. Some of them are so young, they don't even know it's a bus. They think it's another room!

And it's so impersonal. The driver doesn't know from names— numbers! He needs one from this house, two from that one. It can be the father but who cares? As long as he's got the right T-shirt!

Mark my words, we're gonna regret this. I already know kids who look on mother as their nighttime counselor!

DEFINITIONS

For those of you who aren't familiar with baptism, it's sort of a damp *bar mizvah*.

BATHROOM SCALE: something you stand on and swear at.

BERMUDA SHORTS: what your wallet has after a vacation there.

You know what a bigamist is. That's an Italian fog.

BUDGET: a method for going broke methodically.

CHILD'S DEFINITION OF A TEACHER: a nonviolent mother.

Have you noticed how all religions seem to have the same basic ceremonies? For instance, Protestants have confirmations. These are no-cal *bar mizvahs*.

DECEMBER 26TH: when kids start telling you what they want for next Christmas.

Naïveté is calling up Guy Lombardo and asking him if he's doing anything on New Year's Eve.

Nevada proverb: "Show me a man who can lose $2,000, get up from the table, and laugh—and I will show you a shill!"

PASSING ON CURVES: what a beauty-contest judge does.

Patience is a surfer sitting in Walden Pond.

PROSTITUTE: someone who sleeps using the Buddy System.

SHOW AND TELL—what a great name for a lecture by Gypsy Rose Lee!

STRETCH PANTS: sounds like something Lassie does when the show runs under.

UNDERSEXED: someone who notices your *Playboy* calendar is from last year.

DEMONSTRATIONS

Did I have a wild date last night! At two o'clock in the morning, this girl goes on a protest march. Got out of the car and walked home!

For those of you who don't know what a protest march is—it's a Letter to the Editor with blisters.

In Boston a woman was watching a demonstration from her town house and she saw this sign saying: RECOGNIZE RED CHINA! She said: "Recognize Red China! I don't even talk to the maid!"

I won't say the nut groups are involved but one marcher came up with the deadliest threat of all: FLUORIDATE RED CHINA!

I love those signs saying: MAKE LOVE, NOT WAR! I'm married. I do both!

There's only one trouble with signing up for MAKE LOVE, NOT WAR! You're too tired to picket!

Have you taken a good look at these kids who say: MAKE LOVE, NOT WAR! Most of them look like they'd flunk at either.

It's amazing what some of these demonstrators look like. One of them was mentioned three times in one of the greatest military songs ever written: "Tramp, Tramp, Tramp, the Boys Are Marching!"

And these college demonstrations are really something. I went up to one kid and said: "Do you go to this college?" He said: "No." I said: "Do you belong to a political party?" He said: "No." I said: "Do you go to any college?" He said: "No." I said: "Do you have a job?" He said: "No." I said: "Well, what are you protesting?" He said: "Noninvolvement!"

They were supposed to have a big demonstration today, but they had to call it off. Somebody forgot the guitars.

Students are a large part of these demonstrations, but some of them have been away from their classes so long it's a little embarrassing. Yesterday they held a TEECH-IN.

And sit-ins. They're very popular too. That's the problem. Kids are spending four years in college and most of the time they're using the wrong end!

I'm not putting down these student demonstrations. Actually, I think they do the students a lot of good. They're like a meaningful panty raid.

Do you realize if it wasn't for picketing, some kids wouldn't walk at all?

I know a fella who scrimped and saved to send his daughter to high school, to college, to ballet school. Now he's got the only kid who pickets on tippy toes!

I know a kid who spends so much time carrying a picket sign, he's got a navel this wide (INDICATE WITH HANDS)!

Another kid is carrying a picket sign with nothing on it. He's against but he isn't sure what.

I know one student who spends so much time picketing, twenty-five years from now he's gonna want his kids to have all the things he never had—like an education!

One day nine hundred kids went limp. Somebody must have asked them to help with the dishes.

I was talking to one college kid and I asked him: "Do you go in for athletics much?" He said: "Well, I'm an end." I said: "An end on the football team?" He said: "No, an end. I sit-in a lot!"

What with the peace marches and the sit-ins and the ban-the-bomb demonstrations, I know one student who's really doing something unusual. He's going to school.

They say these student demonstrations are a going proposition. I think it's all that beer they drink.

58

But it's amazing how kids can be so concerned over atom bombs, nuclear war, air pollution—everything but the size of the phone bill.

Now there's a new service for students at Berkeley. It's called DIAL-A-SWEAR!

Did you hear about the interior decorator who joined one of the demonstrations? He didn't go limp but his wrist did.

On Madison Avenue six account executives are carrying signs: MAKE MONEY, NOT WAVES!

Some of these protesters have shown up in so many different parts of the country—I'm beginning to believe the pro part of it.

Now they're having demonstrations against demonstrations. One side wants to BAN THE BOMB—the other wants to BAN THE BOOB.

Personally, I don't pretend to have all the answers. If I did, I'd be a student at Berkeley.

DENTISTS

Things aren't bad enough, now there's a scientific report that says kissing causes cavities. I guess that's why they say: "Kiss me— you fool!"

Kissing causes cavities! You could make a fortune with this report. All you gotta be is a combination dentist and divorce lawyer!

One fella came home from the dentist with forty-five cavities. He said to his wife: "I can explain everything, dear. They're from too much sugar." She said: "So that's what you call her!"

Ever since they found out about kissing, you know who's saying: "Look, Ma, no cavities"? Pa!

It's gonna revolutionize the ads: Does she or doesn't she? Only her dentist knows for sure!

Yesterday a dentist's wife walked into his office and found him kissing this ravishing blonde. He looked up and said: "Don't worry, dear. It's business." She said: "Yours or hers?"

All I gotta say is, if kissing causes cavities, in Washington there's gonna be cavities in the wildest places!

Reincarnation is believing that when the Marquis de Sade died, he came back as your dentist.

I don't feel bad about losing my teeth. I figure if God had wanted my teeth to stay in, instead of gums, He would have given me Polident!

DIETING

Now there's a diet that guarantees you'll lose ten pounds a week. It's called the Impacted Molar Diet!

I went on that Drinking Man's Diet and I wanna tell you, it's great. Lost six pounds and three weekends!

According to the Drinking Man's Diet, anything loaded with alcohol and fat is okay. It has to be. I'm married to one!

Some people call it the Drinking Man's Diet. Some call it the Air Force Diet. Either way you wind up flying!

They've even got a Dieter's Cocktail. Three, and you look thin and talk thick!

Talk about embarrassing moments. Last week a fella was dieting so good, a Salvation Army Band was standing around him! . . . He's either gonna have to give up dieting or get his knees half-soled! . . .

Do you realize, if this idea works, what it's gonna do to this country? A hundred and ninety million skinny drunks!

Sir Francis Bacon said it: "Reading maketh a full man." So doth eating Metrecal cookies!

I wish they wouldn't keep talking about the perfection of nature. If it's so perfect, why didn't it put Metrecal in potatoes instead of starch?

DISK JOCKEY LINES

We will now pause for station identification: It's brick, two stories high, and has a green roof. You can't miss it.

I'm getting a little worried about this station. Last week I gave a time check and it bounced.

Isn't that sweet? Someone wrote in and said that I was a unique personality. And look how they spelled unique—E-U-N-U-C-H.

If you stop to think about it, we really do a job for our listeners. Thanks to our commercials, you can get the latest in headache remedies. And thanks to our records, you can get the latest in headaches!

Be sure to tune in tomorrow cause we're having one of the truly big shows of the year. A fourteen-hour telethon to buy eyeballs for Little Orphan Annie!

I don't wanna knock anybody, but it's amazing how many deejay shows these days are recorded, are recorded, are recorded, are recorded.

This is Station —— covering the heart of (YOUR CITY) and the liver and gall bladder of (SUBURB) and (SUBURB).

A lot of people have asked me how I can play all these rock 'n' roll records day after day, week after week, month after month. It really isn't so difficult. All it requires is tolerance, understanding, greed, and good earplugs. . . . So if you've got a complaint, please don't call the station. All I can hear is small H-bombs and my mother-in-law.

For those of you who don't remember my name, tune out! I hate ingrates!

61

It's been such a hot day, we felt we wanted to do something to help. So for the next half-hour, instead of music, you'll hear the soothing, uninterrupted rumble of the studio air conditioner. . . . This is your golden opportunity. Turn us up real loud, close all the windows, and impress the neighbors like mad!

Coming up, a brief pause for station remuneration. (SPIN A COMMERCIAL.)

All over the country, talk shows are taking the place of music shows—and the next record will explain why.

I once had a show that went on at four in the morning. It was for farmers, and I said clever and witty things—like: "WAKE UP!"

They wanted to call the show "Bright and Early," but I was rarely either.

You've heard of records that are 33⅓, 45, and 78? Now they've got one that's 115. It doesn't sound any better but it's over quicker!

Hi, this is ——, your friendly neighborhood disk jockey. And I am friendly. I smile so much I'm the only fella in town with sunburned teeth!

This is Station (YOUR CALL LETTERS)—(YOUR CALL LETTERS), four letters that spell entertainment—and the way they're teaching nowadays, it might!

I don't wanna brag, but this is the first program to feature the big beat. I know it's the first program. I just celebrated the fifth anniversary of my headache.

We've got a great show planned for you tonight. First comes the Top Ten. Then comes the Top Forty. Then comes the Top One Hundred. Then comes the Top Five Hundred. Then comes October!

This is (YOUR CALL LETTERS)—a 50,000-watt station. That may not mean much to you but it makes (LOCAL ELECTRIC UTILITY) pretty happy. Every time we plug in, their stock goes up three points!

We're gonna have a swingin' time tonight. We'll play a whole bunch of your favorite records—plus a few with tunes.

This happens to be a 5,000-watt station. Every time I ask for a raise they say: "What?"

This ends our five-hour show for today. I'd like to do more but the A.S.P.C.A. won't allow it.

Gosh, I just love playing these records. Why, if this wasn't a job, I'd do it for nothing. And every time I get my paycheck, I think I am. . . . I've heard of small pay checks, but I think mine are transistorized.

Isn't that a great sound? And that's just the cover. Wait'll you hear the record!

Now we've gathered together forty-three different versions of (POPULAR OVERPLAYED CHRISTMAS RECORD) and as a special Christmas treat, we're not gonna play them.

Wasn't that a great record? "Santa Claus Is Coming to Town?" Last year he showed up January 3rd. Took the (LOCAL COMMUTER BUS OR TRAIN).

Bing Crosby's still dreaming of a "White Christmas." I'm a *Playboy* man myself.

I just figured out what that group gave up for Lent—rehearsals!

I always have one great fear while playing that record. If the Russians ever attacked, we'd never know it!

I think it's orchestrated for piano, sax, bass, and Nike missile.

We dedicate this next record to the barbers of America—those courageous, unsung, unflinching, unappreciated men who, year after year, offer this country the ultimate in self-sacrifice. Do you realize there are over 600,000 hairs on your head—and they cut every cotton-picking one of them for a lousy buck and a half? . . . I don't care what your business is. Would you do it

63

600,000 times for a buck and a half? . . . This is a rhetorical question so please don't write. Really. I've never seen such faithful listeners. Last week I said: "How 'bout that?"—and 28 of you wrote in to tell me!

That was —— a record never to be forgotten—provided the world ends at midnight.

AFTER A WILD RECORD: Believe me, there's nothing like fine, outstanding music—especially on this program.

A little song entitled: "Let Me Call You Sweetheart, I've Called You Everything Else."

That was the —— first release—although I'm not really sure it was released. I think it escaped!

Sometimes I wonder if I'm not getting too progressive for this business. Instead of radio, maybe I oughta be on radar!

That's a pretty wild record. Sounds like a pizza played at 33⅓!

That was: "When Your Hair Has Turned to Silver, You'll Have the Most Expensive Wig in Town."

You haven't lived until you've heard Ed Sullivan's LP. First time I ever heard knuckles cracked to Cole Porter.

THIS IS MY FIRST AFFAIR, SO PLEASE BE KIND. Wouldn't that make a great graduation song for a catering school?

DISCOTHEQUES

Is it true there's a discotheque in Fort Wayne, Indiana, that features Hoosier Hot Shot records?

Down in Hot Springs they have a discotheque that only serves mineral water. It's called GO GO A GO GO!

I know a woman who spent $500 on dancing lessons. Learned the Frug, the Jerk, the Watusi, but she still didn't move right. Then she spent three more dollars and now she's the hit of the discotheques. Bought a wool girdle!

It's all right to be uninhibited, but who does (CURRENT DANCE) to "Ave Maria"?

It's a very unusual dance. The only thing you don't move is your feet!

Picture a hundred dancers carrying on like they did in those 1930 pictures—just before they cut to Vesuvius erupting!

And they always have two or three girl dancers on a platform above the crowd. I don't know what they're doing, but they look like cheerleaders in a bawdyhouse!

These aren't dances. They're fertility rites with lyrics!

I don't wanna put down discotheques—but one of them opened up on a street that had four horse rooms, three saloons, and six strip joints—and someone said: "Well, there goes the neighborhood!"

And if you're over forty, do yourself a favor and stay out of discotheques. 'Cause at this age it's no longer dancing. It's committing suicide one bone at a time!

I think the whole gimmick to these dances is to have an itch where you can't scratch!

I saw one woman, fifty-five years old, doing an unbelievably wild step. I said: "That's marvelous. Do you come here often?" She said: "First time." I said: "First time? How did you ever learn to dance like that?" She said: "What dance? Where's the ladies' room?"

It's nice to know the night clubs haven't lost their sense of humor. One place has six topless dancers and what do you think they're down on the payroll as? Bouncers!

I don't know why they keep referring to these girls as topless. Anybody who considers these girls topless—is spoiled!

Remember the good old days, when people danced cheek to cheek, instead of kneecap to kneecap?

DRINKING

I got an idea that's gonna make me a fortune. Sen Sen-flavored booze!

It was so cold last night, I did something I've always wanted to do. Took a quart of scotch, poured it into ice trays, put it outside my hotel window, and let it freeze. For months my doctor has been bugging me with: "You're thirsty? Fill up a glass with seltzer—and if you gotta add something, what's wrong with ice cubes?" . . . Doc, not a darn thing!

Now there's a group that wants to fluoridate martinis—so you won't get holes in your teeth, just your liver.

Suffer from hangovers in the morning? Tried our aspirin-flavored bourbon? . . . I won't say what the bourbon does to the aspirin, but when it finally does catch up to the Bufferin, it kicks the hell out of it!

Drinking beer has become such an adventure these days. Sometimes you open the can with your fingers—and sometimes you open your fingers with the can.

Have you tried those self-opening beer cans, or don't you like the taste of blood?

I won't say those self-opening beer cans are dangerous, but the blood bank closed all its regular offices. Now they just stand around bars with a bucket.

Have you ever tried to open one of these things? They made only one mistake. They put beer inside and it should have been iodine. . . . I bought a can the other day and it's the first time I ever lost two pints to drink one! . . . You know those handy six-packs? They don't come wrapped in cardboard any more—tourniquets!

There's a rumor going around that Alcoholics Anonymous is working on self-closing beer cans.

People have the strangest sense of humor. Like, I wonder how many potted plants are sent to Alcoholics Anonymous each year?

Alcoholics Anonymous is so strict, they won't even let their members watch Dean Martin!

Remember the good old days—when beer foamed and dishwater didn't?

DRIVING

"What you don't know won't hurt you!"—is a very profound statement—as anyone who has ever lingered to watch an attendant park his car has found out.

I watched one yesterday and I didn't know you could coast forward in reverse.

And the way they back the car in—you know, with the door open? That's so they can dent the upholstery too!

It's amazing the things you see on the roads these days. I saw a fella driving one of these little sports cars and he's playing a guitar. I pulled up alongside and said: "Pardon me, sir—but do you know you're an affront and a mockery to the traffic laws of our great and sovereign state?" (PANTOMIME HOLDING A GUITAR.) He said: "No. How does it go?"

DRUGS

They call LSD a consciousness-expanding drug. I got news. At six o'clock in the morning, a consciousness-expanding drug is coffee.

Then there's low-cal LSD. It's for people who want their consciousness expanded but not very much!

There's a group that wants to legalize marijuana and they've got a wonderful slogan: "SMOKE COOL! SMOKE COOL!"

To get support for legalized marijuana, they're flying all over the country. And they don't even have a plane!

Actually, you can always tell people who smoke marijuana by their living rooms. The couch has safety belts!

E

EDUCATION

I'm against sex education in the schools. What kids need today is sex ignoration—for a few more years than they have it.

One of the first things a child seems to learn when he goes to school is that other kids are getting a bigger allowance than he is.

School kids today are fantastic. They don't exactly drink at the fountain of knowledge. They just sort of gargle a little.

I have a great idea that's gonna completely eliminate the dropout problem. We just make hookey a major!

This no Bible reading is tough enough on public schools—but can you imagine what it's doing to divinity schools?

A science column had a wonderful piece of advice. It said: "The way to see an eclipse is to punch a hole in a piece of cardboard, hold it over another piece of cardboard, stand with your back to the burning sun, and let us know what happens." A reader sent in a one-word answer: "Sunstroke!" . . . Tell the truth now. Did you get the same reaction to the eclipse that I got? It's a lot like a honeymoon. Sounds a lot more exciting than it actually is!

Things are happening so fast, history books are adding a chapter a week.

Basically, there are two types of math you can learn in school. The New Math—if you want to be creative, imaginative, and forward-thinking. And the Old Math—if you want to be right.

I know a fella who's a bigamist and it isn't his fault. With the New Math, what does he know?

Isn't it wonderful? Summer's over—and your kids are finally going back to someone who can handle them.

We found a wonderful private school for ours—The Mafia School for Moppets . . . straight A's or straitjackets.

The government wants to give grants to teachers. They don't need grants. They just need a whip, a chair, and a gun!

I don't know whether we should encourage teachers to get any more education. They get any smarter than they are, and they'll get into something that pays!

Now everybody's talking about Educational Parks—a single cluster of buildings where you can go from kindergarten to public school to junior high school to senior high school to college to graduate school to Medicare!

Actually, the idea of Educational Parks is nothing new. You walk through Central Park after midnight and right away you learn one thing. Don't walk through Central Park after midnight!

I'm for sex education—but not for teen-agers—for parents. That way when they look at their kids and say: "What did we do to deserve this?" they'll know!

ELECTIONS

I'm fascinated by these fund-raising dinners that cost $1,000 a plate. One fella paid $1,000 and ate like there was no tomorrow. And when that check bounces, there won't be!

I didn't mind the $1,000 a plate so much. It was the $5.00 each for Tums!

We're approaching election time again, when candidates all over the country are saying: STOP THE WORLD, I WANT TO GET IN!

You know, I finally figured out why they call them primaries. It's the age level most of the speeches are aimed at.

I'll say this about the candidates. They're both trying to put their best foot forward. It's getting it out of their mouth that's the problem.

In some ways (CANDIDATE) is like a cat. He's licking himself with his own tongue.

They've just created a martini based on (CANDIDATE's) chances —8 to 1.

I know each of the candidates has a brain trust, but after hearing some of these speeches, you just wonder if "trust" shouldn't be spelled with two s's.

One doctor has a new cure for insomnia. Drink a warm glass of milk; take a hot bath; then listen to (CANDIDATE).

Is this man a speaker? Even when he coughs he sounds like he's reading!

I'm really worried about one of the candidates. His idea of subtlety is: Fee, fie, foe, fum—(OPPOSING CANDIDATE) is a bum!

Personally, I have a Chinese restaurant attitude toward this election. I just want (NAME OF CANDIDATE)—to go!

They took this survey in ten leading colleges, asking students: "If you had the opportunity to be (UNPOPULAR LEADER) at this moment—what would you want most?" One of them answered: "Another opportunity."

Election Day: the day millions of Americans go to the polls to determine which political analyst was right!

Did you ever run into Election Day Stereo? When the Democrat sound truck is on one corner and the Republican sound truck is on the other? . . . And you're in the middle getting that bipartisan migraine?

Whatever happens to all those sound trucks between elections? If Tarzan ever finds the elephants' graveyard, he can work on this next.

Maybe we oughta increase the stakes in these elections. Like the one who loses has to take down all the posters on lampposts.

I'll say one thing about the politicians I've seen on TV. They don't lie any more than the average sponsor.

Political speeches on TV are getting such low ratings, we may have the first national election ever to be pre-empted by an old movie.

The —th Congress just opened and you notice how they always call them by numbers? It's shrewd. Like I know a fella who's been married to the same woman for thirty-five years and yet he still calls her his first wife. Claims it keeps her on her toes!

Behind every President of the United States there stands a proud wife—and a mother-in-law saying: "He couldn't be an accountant and come home nights?"

EMCEE LINES

Things are happening so fast, I've had three acts go out of style in the last twenty minutes.

I don't get many laughs with my material but the smiles are deafening!

I got a little suspicious of my last writer when he told me he was doing ad-libs for Marcel Marceau.

I love the way this audience really joins in. This isn't so much a show as group therapy with drinks!

Hey, everybody who didn't get loaded New Year's Eve, raise their hands. How about everybody who didn't get loaded New Year's Day? The day after New Year's Day? . . . That's what I thought. You're my kind of drunks!

ABOUT THE BAND: It's embarrassing going out with these fellas. Like last Sunday we went to this big church downtown. A tremendous choir; a soloist with the voice of an angel. Amidst this cathedral hush, she sings the most beautiful version of "*Ave Maria*" I've ever heard. Comes to the closing, awe-inspiring few bars—the drummer, what's-his-name there, stands up and yells: "One more time!"

We're gonna try to keep the show impromptu tonight. That's show-business for disorganized.

I won't say what I'm getting paid in this place, but name me one other comedian who borrows money from schoolteachers?

Professional comedians have the same problems as the world's oldest profession. It isn't the hours that ruin you, it's the amateur competition!

Personally, I'm 90 per cent behind the President. The other 10 per cent belongs to my agent.

I'm very proud 'cause as of three o'clock this afternoon, I finally memorized my Zip Code, my Area Code, my Social Security number, and my unlisted telephone number. 'Course, I forgot my act.

CLOSING: I'd like to do more but my twenty-four-hour deodorant is giving out.

ENGLAND

Isn't it amazing how dignified all those British politicians are? You get the impression they could remain aloof during a prostate examination.

Two society women were watching the Queen and one said: "Breeding is everything, isn't it?" The other woman said: "No, but it's lots of fun!"

It's an amazing thing watching the Royal Family. They're so poised, so charming, so gracious—did you ever get the feeling Benedict Arnold might have been right?

I never realized how shy the English are. Do you realize on British beaches they use handshake to handshake resuscitation?

You remember England—where the change-of-pace drink is coffee. . . . I won't say what it tastes like, but you know Madame Tussaud's Chamber of Horrors? The first one is a cup of English coffee.

I don't blame the British for wanting their own nuclear striking force. Any country that does to coffee, beer, and food what these people do—needs to be able to defend itself.

They say we've got a lot in common with the British but I dunno. Any country where the Breakfast of Champions is kippered herring (SHAKE YOUR HEAD).

Sports cars are very popular in England. The British don't really need big, powerful cars 'cause most of their roads are small, narrow, and twisting. A freeway in England is anything that lets you get into third.

The last time I was in England I got a ticket—for going 12 miles an hour in an 8-mile zone.

The sun never sets on the British Empire. It can't. It's too busy looking for it!

I hear the British are forming their own N.A.A.C.P. The National Association for the Advancement of Crumbling Powers.

I won't say they're going to pieces, but it's a good thing for England there's no such thing as a Used-Country Lot.

Suddenly the entire British Empire seems to be coming apart at the seams. I feel if Rudyard Kipling were alive today, he'd be writing for *Playboy*.

EXTREMISTS

Two extremists were watching the first act of *A Christmas Carol* on television. One of them nudges the other, points at Scrooge, and says: "That boy's talking real sense!"

Did you hear about the bigot who was accused of beating, burning, maiming, and murder—and he got very upset. Threw down his robe and said: "That does it! From now on—no more Mr. Nice Guy!"

They're really something. One yelled: "Go back to Russia, ya dirty, lousy Communist rat fink, ya! No offense intended."

Remember the good old days—when an extremist group was people who brushed after every meal?

Then there's an organization called the Minute Men. I won't say anything about the Minute Men—although I do feel a little sorry for their wives.

It's fascinating how many different political groups are forming. Pretty soon every little meaning will have a movement all its own.

There's a group that wants to make everything in this country 100 per cent American. Like we won't call them English muffins any more—Boston bagels. . . . And Russian roulette will be known as Mississippi monopoly.

I just found out why some of these trials take so long. One lawyer stutters and every time he says "K.K.K."—there goes the morning!

I've often wondered why they picked a sheet as their trademark. Somehow a crazy quilt seems more appropriate.

Personally, I'm fascinated by those sheets. All they gotta do is climb into bed and they're in uniform!

But you can't put down everyone in the Klan. I saw one fella who was pretty hip. You could tell. He was the only one who wore his sheet four inches above the knee.

Did you know the Ku Klux Klan has a branch in San Francisco? First time I ever saw a topless sheet!

They're finding out that a lot of the racist leaders are living off the fatheads of the land.

One is making so much money, he's got a vicuna sheet!

Progress to some people is split-level slave quarters.

I wonder what tremists were like before they changed?

F

FADS

The kids have a new craze. One of them stayed in a shower 33 hours, 33 minutes and 33 seconds. He would have stayed in longer only—that would have been silly.

Thirty-three hours in a hot shower. I don't know if he's studying to be a doctor or a tea bag!

Let's face it, when this kid leaves his mark on the world I think I know what it's gonna be—a puddle!

But can you imagine what thirty-three hours in a shower does to you? You come out looking like you talked back to a witch doctor!

It's ridiculous. I wouldn't spend this long in a shower if Brigitte Bardot was the sponge!

This fella's skin was so dry, someone snapped him with a towel and he tore!

FALL

Doesn't this weather do something to you? The air is just alive with the smell of burning leaves, apple cider, and mothballs.

Isn't it interesting the way leaves turn yellow, red, and golden as they get older? Just like women.

October is when the greens turn to browns and our tans turn to pales.

I don't wanna criticize Mother Nature, but wouldn't it have been a lot smarter to have leaves fall *up?*

77

October is Surprise Month. When you zip open the plastic bags, pull out the clothes, and see which worked—the moths or the moth balls.

Everybody seems to get their clothes out the same time. "Darling, you smell delicious tonight. Chanel No. 5?" "No. Black Flag No. 9!"

I love this time of year. Going home in the autumn twilight—smelling things burning. Not leaves, lamb chops. My wife's a terrible cook!

Autumn is that magic time of the year when you look out and the pool is no longer filled with your neighbors' kids. It's filled with your neighbors' leaves.

October 1st is when all trees look like the Beatles. Comes November 1st—Yul Brynner!

The big problem with autumn is by the time you've raked up the leaves, put up the storm windows, and emptied out the pool—it ain't!

Here it is fall again—when teachers all over the country are quitting their summer jobs to go back to their winter jobs!

AUTUMN: when the bare limbs go from the girls to the trees.

FANNY HILL

I didn't realize what a wild town this was until I found out they don't put copies of the Bible in hotel rooms—*Fanny Hill!*

Have you read *Fanny Hill?* I won't say what she did for a living, but when you get the book home, the jacket comes off by itself.

Fanny Hill was an eighteenth-century call girl who really had it rough—no phone!

'Course, in those days they didn't call them call girls—courtesans! Courtesan—isn't that a wonderful word? If you introduced a girl to a cop today as a courtesan, he'd probably bow.

I'm really amazed at some of the books they're putting out these days. I read one yesterday—picture a dirty *Fanny Hill.*

FATHER'S DAY

For those of you unfamiliar with Father's Day—it's sort of a Discount Mother's Day.

Father's Day is a device that gives tens of thousands of druggists all over the country a chance to get rid of the shaving sets they couldn't move at Christmas . . . you know the sets I mean: 20¢ worth of shaving cream, 15¢ worth of after-shave lotion, 10¢ worth of talcum—and $2.00 worth of box.

And the boxes always have a picture on them—like the head of a horse, or a dog, or fishing tackle. Something masculine. And you need this—'cause after you put on that lotion, people aren't so sure. . . . I know some kids who gave their dad a lotion like this. Father liked it so much, he's now their mother!

The talcum is interesting. Guaranteed to clog the pores in your skin. Fortunately, it also clogs the holes in the can so you never get to find this out.

You know what makes a great Father's Day present? An electric shaver! 'Cause if Mother doesn't use it, Sister will. . . . With each passing year, a new type of Togetherness is being created. The family who shaves together, stays together!

FLORIDA

I know a fella who had an embarrassing experience. He told his boss he was going into a hospital for an operation and then spent two weeks in Florida. But when he got back, his color gave him away.
Tan?
Blue.

I had some Florida orange juice this morning. It came prechilled, but that isn't why I knew it came from Florida—the pits were shivering.

Incidentally, if you have friends in Florida paying $50 a day for the coldest sun this side of Norway—why don't you bug 'em a little? There's a store next door selling fur-lined cabana sets.

I love Florida during the hurricane season. Where else can you get a ticket for going 85 miles an hour—and never leave your house?

FLU

Do you realize that when a flu germ says: "There's a lot of it going around!"—he means penicillin?

There's only one difference between paying a call on royalty and getting a penicillin shot. When you visit royalty, you back *out*.

One doctor did nothing but give penicillin shots for five straight days. Then he went berserk! He said: "I can't take it any more! It's like being a midget in a nudist parade!"

I'm really getting worried. Yesterday I heard an aspirin talking to a Bufferin outside my bloodstream. It was saying: "Me? Go into *that?*"

The first thing to remember during any flu epidemic is—never go near your mailman. He's a carrier.

Every time I get the sniffles, I always curl up with a good book, a good bottle, and a bad blonde. It's the only way to flu!

Believe me, there's only way to avoid the sniffles. Drink lots of water. Lots of water! Let's face it—when have you ever seen a fish with a cold?

And these colds are spreading to the whole country. Yesterday I had cereal for breakfast and it was going: "Snap! Crackle! Sniff!"

Five million Americans are suffering from the Hong Kong flu. I think it's the Hong Kong flu. Everybody is saying: "Ah Chou!"

With the cold weather here, millions of Americans are coming down with the same thing—politician's flu. It's from spending too much time in rooms filled with hot air!

FLYING SAUCERS

I don't believe in flying saucers. I only saw a flying saucer once—when a nudist spilled hot coffee in his lap.

Did you ever get the feeling that, when it comes to flying saucers, the Air Force makes up its denials six months in advance?

Personally, I think we are being watched by people from outer space. I also think they're going to contact the responsible leaders of Earth—just as soon as they can find one.

FOLK SONGS

They say folk music is the living expression of a people. What people do you know who spend their lives stomping on the floor and singing through their nose?

It's always fascinating to hear a seventeen-year-old kid sing about the Wabash Cannonball. He doesn't even remember trolley cars!

I'm not putting the younger generation down—but sometimes, work songs are as close as some of them ever get to it.

One group has taken to updating folk songs. Like in their version of that famous railroad song—"Casey Jones isn't trying to make up time. He's trying to make up the deficit."

Frankly, I'm a little suspicious of all these authentic folk songs they're digging up. At latest count, there's at least 18,742,000 folk songs around. And a hundred years ago, there weren't even that many folk!

I'm not knocking folk singers, mind you. Anyone who can turn an adenoid condition into a million dollars, earns my respect!

Did you hear about that new folk group? It's four fathers and they sing protest songs about phone bills!

I know a folk singer who's making a fortune singing freedom songs in Leavenworth.

You know who fascinate me? Girl folk singers. Wool sweater, wool skirt, wool stockings. Last night one of them was attacked by a moth!

They stand there with the yellow and white make-up on and the black eye shadow. You don't know if they're sexy or contagious!

I know one who happens to be a three-letter girl in college—U-G-H!

I happen to know that all girl folk singers are faced with the same two problems. Getting boys to take them out—and keeping cats from dragging them in!

And the big thing with all these student demonstrators is folk songs. Simple tunes with simple thoughts that take us back to the days when life was uncomplicated; when men plowed the earth for their daily bread; when World Wars were unknown; when children were seen and not heard.

FOREIGN AFFAIRS

It's interesting the way the Germans look on us. They don't think of this as the United States. It's where the Volkswagens go.

You wanna know the reason that Berlin Wall is still standing? My wife doesn't drive a car there!

I happen to know that if attacked—Israel has the heaviest, the most dangerous, the most impenetrable missile ever devised by mortal man! A two-week-old bagel!

That's the big new secret weapon. They're gonna load up a plane with these bagels, go up to 10,000 feet, drop them on Nasser—and if the bagels don't do it, the lox fallout will!

It's no wonder modern Egypt is having such a tough time of it. I mean, how far would Nasser get, rolling out of a rug naked?

I dig Rhodesia. I figure, any country that can make Alabama look liberal can't be all bad!

In fact, in my mind's eye, I know just what Rhodesia looks like. It's Mississippi with lions!

India doesn't have much in the way of industry, but it does have six hundred million people. Well, it's nice to know they're good at something!

The only time it pays to be neutral today, is when your wife and mother-in-law argue.

You know what I don't understand? Anything that happens in any foreign country—right away students attack the United States embassy. Like it was the thing to do. The weatherman predicts rain. Attack the U.S. embassy! A waiter spills coffee in your lap. Attack the U.S. embassy! . . . It's like these people have an Edifice Complex.

Washington is involved in so many things. Did you know they were working on a prefabricated U.S. embassy building for the smaller Asian countries? Comes with the windows already broken.

I'm gonna join the diplomatic corps. You can hardly pick up a paper without reading about some U.S. embassy getting stoned.

I don't know why everybody's saying we don't have a foreign policy. We most certainly do have a foreign policy. Shorter wars but more of them!

Do you realize that since this economic-aid program got started, we've given away a hundred billion dollars? America's the only country where Santa Claus comes just once a year.

American foreign aid has created a situation unique in the history of morals—kept countries!

FRANCE

The French are aiming their newest antialcoholic campaign at kids. We're trying to keep them off the streets and they're trying to keep them off the sauce. . . . According to a recent survey, 85 per cent of all kids aged fourteen and fifteen drink either wine or beer. The rest were too drunk to answer. . . . I'll bet their school lunches must be wild affairs. These are the only kids who carry their own coasters!

Paris is really a swingin' town. Where else can you go to fundraising orgies? . . . Really, you have no idea. First time I ever saw pornographic stained-glass windows.

I can't understand why we're having all this trouble with France. Let's face it, the French and Americans have always had the same interests—broads! . . . I don't blame the West for being shook. I've always considered France the Texas of Europe—where never is heard a discouraging word. . . . Here's an entire country dedicated to the proposition—and suddenly they're saying no!

I'm so mad at France, I'm drawing clothes on the postcards!

The American colony in Paris is doing a patriotic thing. They're still sitting in the first ten rows of the Folies-Bergère—but now they're yawning.

For those of you unfamiliar with the Folies-Bergère, it's sort of a naked discotheque!

You've gotta hand it to the French. They've just updated Cinderella. Instead of a slipper, they're using a bra.

You know what I like about France? Where else can you buy *Fanny Hill* as a coloring book? . . . My name is Fanny. Color me often!

Have you noticed there's one basic difference between British and French movies? In British movies they say: "How do I love thee? Let me count the ways." In French movies, they show them.

As far as I'm concerned, the French have always had their own independent deterrent—garlic!

De Gaulle keeps saying the French can take care of themselves. And they can—except during wars.

Do you realize that in the last sixty years, the only foreigners the French have been able to drive out are American tourists?

GADGETS

Someone gave me an electric toothbrush for Christmas. Unfortunately, I've got wind-up teeth!

You gotta be careful with electric toothbrushes. Why, the major cause of halitosis in America today is weak batteries!

Remember the good old days, when radios plugged in and toothbrushes didn't?

I have one of those Early American Electric Toothbrushes. Comes with a key, a kite, and it only works during thunderstorms!

And you really gotta watch the kids with electric toothbrushes. I saw my five-year-old holding his in a glass. I said: "What's that?" He said: "A Pepsodent malted!"

There's only one thing that shakes me about these electric toothbrushes. Did you ever figure to see the day when you'd make a down payment on a toothbrush?

But it's really wonderful owning an electric toothbrush. You see your dentist twice a year and your electrician once a month!

A lot of people think the electric toothbrush is silly, but it really isn't. Along with the electric dishwasher, the electric can opener, and the power shoehorn—it's become a vital part of the American scene!

Pretty soon we're going to be a transistorized, battery-operated, muscleless society. Yesterday a kid showed up for his first Little League game. They gave him a bat and he wanted to know where to plug it in.

Then with progressive education, they ran into another problem. In the third inning they got eleven runs. Who can count that high? They hadda get a pinch scorer!

But it's the electric toothbrush I'm fascinated by. What if the brush is A.C. and your teeth are D.C.?

I just don't agree with those people who think an electric toothbrush is decadent. And neither does my bath maid.

Right now, in our bathroom, we have an electric toothbrush, an electric razor, an electric sun lamp, an electric hair dryer, an electric massager. We got more controls in the john than they used to get Frankenstein swingin'. . . . Never mind, can your wife cook? What does she know about fuses? . . . A real catch today isn't a homemaker. It's an electrical engineer!

Personally, I think I just reached the ultimate in status symbols. A power mower with a stick shift.

You wanna know how wars start? Take a wife with an electric coffee maker, a husband with an electric razor, a son with an electric guitar, and a daughter with an electric hair dryer—and put 'em all together in a house with one outlet.

I can see it now. Hundreds of years from now, archaeologists poking around in the dust of what once was New York—trying to determine what caused the decline and fall of the American civilization. And all they can find is a battery-operated pepper mill.

GARDENING

We had a terrible night last night. The tree doctor came over at two in the morning and put our spruce on the critical list. . . . But if you ever need a tree doctor, I gotta recommend this man. He has a real trunkside manner. . . . The way he stands there, holding a branch and looking at his watch.

Then he turns to you and utters those dreaded words: "Dry rot!" "Doctor, what can save it?" "Money!" . . . I won't say how much

I've spent, but last year I claimed four dependents on my income tax. A wife, two kids, and a birch! . . . Actually, that's the whole secret of successful gardening today. You gotta have a long green thumb.

Incidentally, if you're not familiar with them, it's very easy to spot a tree doctor. He's the one who double-parks in front of a national forest.

I get so suspicious of those little lanterns you hang outside and they're supposed to attract bugs and kill them. Last year I put eight out and I only caught one bug. And I'm not even sure about him 'cause he left a suicide note.

My wife is crazy for buying plant food. I don't wanna complain, but we've got the only lawn on the block with fat grass!

Personally, I don't believe in feeding lawns. If it's hungry, let it go out and work, like I did!

Be honest now, who else do you know who gives a lawn a two o'clock feeding? . . . It's embarrassing. You take someone out to see the lawn and all it does is sit there, going (BURP)!

Did you hear the latest? No-Cal Fertilizer for Fat Geraniums?

I know I'm gonna have a rough summer. This morning I went out to work on my lawn, and it's the first time I ever heard crab grass singing "We Shall Overcome"!

I think my wife's been lending out our power lawn mower. There's strange blood on it.

GOVERNMENT SPENDING

The government is just finishing its fiscal year. Fiscal year—that's an accounting device that postpones bad news for six months.

Congress increased our debt limit again. It's a new fiscal concept—Government by Diner's Club.

Remember the good old days, when bathing suits were topless instead of the Federal Budget?

They're now calling it the Hemline Budget. Every time they talk about it, it goes higher!

According to the new Federal Budget, there's gonna be something for every man, woman, and child in this country—bankruptcy!

They say the public debt is now $7,190 for every U.S. family. Just our luck World War III starts and someone repossesses the Army!

It's fantastic the way the President is coming up with all these government spending programs. I don't mind stimulating the economy but let's not show it dirty movies!

Remember the good old days—when the only Social Security this country had was Sen Sen?

If the government is really looking for additional revenue, how about charging extra for low Zip Code numbers?

Wouldn't it be great if they put Medicare under the Department of Agriculture? Then people would be paid for not growing an appendix!

Say, I just thought of a way for the Government to save seven billion dollars. Take Medicare out and put Christian Science in!

I love that phrase "pockets of poverty." Sounds like my wife's bra.

Isn't that great? Statistics show that unemployment is down. And you know how they did it? Putting all those people to work compiling unemployment statistics!

A Detroit congressman has an idea that'll save us eight billion dollars in defense spending. We use last year's rockets, but we change the grille a little.

The President really means business about the Government's economizing. Yesterday I got a letter with 6¢ postage due. This morning they attached my salary.

There's so much cutting being done on the new budget, the *Christian Science Monitor* won't even mention it. . . . Six more cuts and the President is gonna have to sign the budget with a styptic pencil.

Congress finally adjourned. I wonder how it feels to be a member of a Congress that spent more than a hundred billion dollars—then go home on an economy flight?

Whoever said "It's not the basic cost, it's the upkeep"—had to be talking about the Government.

HALLOWEEN

H

I just can't wait till Halloween comes around. There'll be this big vat of gibsons—and we'll all bob for onions!

Say, I keep hearing about bobbed noses. What in the world are bobbed noses? Sounds like something you do on Halloween when you run out of apples!

Halloween's the time when little girls love to get dressed up in their mothers' old clothes. Unfortunately, little boys can't get dressed up in their fathers' old clothes—'cause Dad's still wearing them.

Isn't it amazing how expensive Halloween costumes have become? I saw a witch's outfit for $29. I said: "Twenty-nine dollars? That's ridiculous!" The clerk said: "What's so ridiculous? It's made from an imported design, custom-tailored, hand-stitched, and a fine yarn." I said: "Yes, and you tell it well!"

Halloween has certainly changed. When I was a teen-ager, kids would go around whacking each other with stockings filled with flour. Now all the kids are pacifists. They still go around, but it's to negotiate!

And years ago, chalk was a big thing. You'd put a chalk mark on someone's pants and yell: "Halloween!" One kid enjoyed it so much, he became a tailor.

A realistic parent is one who, after 9:00 P.M. on Halloween, stops giving Trick-or-Treaters candy and starts giving them Tums.

I don't know how the jack-o'-lantern ever got to be an American symbol. It fits the Russians so much better. Looks ferocious even when it's smiling at you.

HAWAII

When it comes to races, Hawaii has more varieties than Heinz!

I like Hawaii. Hawaii is the only state I know where the white backlash could hold a meeting in a Volkswagen!

Wouldn't that be wild? A race riot in Hawaii? You'd spend one minute hitting and three hours figuring out *who* to hit!

You can always tell the tourists in Hawaii. They're the ones who go home three shades darker and $2,000 lighter! . . . That is, if they go economy class.

I went to a luau—which is what your lawn party'd look like if the chair-rental service goofed.

It's interesting. In Hawaii they cook over open fires, sit on the ground, eat with their fingers—and they get tourists. In Africa they do the very same thing—and they get the Peace Corps.

It's fascinating eating poi. It's like a fish dip using your finger instead of potato chips.

Everything's made with pineapple of course—drinks, desserts, fortunes. . . . Personally, I think they overdo it. For the next few months, if I hear the phrase "The Yellow Peril"—to me it'll be pineapples.

But it's so exotic drinking out of coconut shells, pineapples, watermelons. What makes it exotic, I was drinking coffee.

And those wonderful rum drinks made with fruit juices. Where else can you find alcoholics with so much vitamin C?

HEALTH FOODS

My wife's on a new kick now. Health foods! Do you know what it is to drink Tiger's Milk eight times a day? Yesterday Tarzan walked by and I bit him!

She's been giving me so much Tiger's Milk I started to get worried. I called up my doctor and said: "Doc, I've been drinking six quarts of Tiger's Milk a day. Is it gonna affect me?" He said: "Would you talk a little louder?" I said: "I can't. I'm in a gas tank!"

And my mother-in-law drinks goat's milk. She's always butting in.

But you know what bothers me about health foods? If they're supposed to be so good, how come every time I go into a health-food store, the guy behind the counter always looks like Don Knotts?

HIPPIES

You've heard of deodorants? Now they've got an odorant. It's for nouveau hippies.

Believe me, it isn't easy being a hippie. How do you think they feel when pools make them wear a bathing cap?

Did you hear about the two Ku Klux Klanners who became hippies? Now when they burn a cross, it's made of driftwood.

LUNATIC FRINGE: what a wonderful name for a hippie haircut!

HOLIDAYS

COLUMBUS DAY: Say, I just had a wild thought. Can you imagine if Columbus hadda been born Frank Sinatra—and he didn't discover America—he sent for it?

I always let the kids dye the Easter eggs, but last year they used the wrong bottle. Instead of artificial food colors, they took something from my wife's dressing table. We had the only peroxide Easter eggs in town.

I always enjoy the Easter eggs with the wavy colored lines. You know the ones I mean? They look like $99 color TV.

JULY 4TH WEEKEND: Incidentally, I want you all to be particularly careful when driving home tonight. It's the last day of a long weekend; the weather is turning nasty; and my wife just asked for the car keys.

That Safety Council is predicting how many people are gonna get it on July 4th again. Don't these fellas have a grim job? It's like being emcee at Armageddon!

Paul Revere, as you may remember, is the one who rode through every Middlesex village and town yelling: "The Redcoats are coming! The Redcoats are coming!" And nobody paid any attention to him. They just figured it was a sale at Robert Hall.

You can't imagine what this beach is like on the 4th of July. Last year they had one drowning and three crushings!

I wonder if fish at summer resorts ever wonder where all the toes go after Labor Day?

ST. PATRICK'S DAY: The reason people in Washington are so fascinated by Ireland—over there, if you have to kiss anything, it's just the Blarney Stone.

HOLLYWOOD

Hollywood is where they have secret weddings and catered divorces.

You gotta give Hollywood credit for trying. Now they've got a starlet who's fat, forty, wears glasses, no make-up, and a baggy old bathrobe. She's a sex symbol for men who no longer care!

The scene is a Hollywood rehearsal hall. A young fella is practicing splits, the time step, the buck and wing. An agent walks up to him and says: "Want to get into show business, kid?" He says: "No. Government!"

You know what I like about Hollywood? Even the churches swing! Where else can you look into a collection plate and see credit cards?

And look at the way the movies have changed. I can remember when the saltiest thing you ever got in a movie was popcorn.

Yesterday I saw a movie that was so embarrassing, I asked the lady in front of me to put her hat back on again.

Did you hear about the fella who went to so many of those wild films—he wanted to get married but he'd already seen the movie!

HORROR MOVIES

Have you been watching those old horror movies on TV? It's unbelievable. They've got Frankenstein, witches, vampires—and you know what gets me? They all live in the suburbs and I'll bet not one of them had any trouble integrating! . . . Which is a good thing, 'cause if the Frankenstein monster and Dracula ever sang "We Shall Overcome," you better believe it!

You don't rent to the count and the next morning you got a thank-you note where your Adam's apple should be!

Now they're working on a TV series about a modern Dracula. In the very first show he bites into a bloodstream and gets two pints and three Bufferin.

Did you hear about the airline that used to show Dracula pictures but no more? After every flight, two little punctures in the gas tank.

It's really wonderful the way they keep trying to update those Frankenstein pictures. Like in the next one they're giving the monster a nude scene.

But you gotta give this fella credit. Let's face it, he's been making movies for thirty-three years now. He is no spring monster. . . . Look real close and you can see he's getting a little gray around the stitches.

I don't mind a middle-aged monster so much. It's when he stops doing this (BUSINESS WITH THE HANDS OVERHEAD AND THE STAGGERING AND THE GROWLING) to take Geritol. . . . Can you imagine having tired blood and it ain't even yours? . . . I don't know who's gonna get him first—the townspeople or Medicare.

And you also gotta admire Baron Frankenstein. Operating forty years and never lost a corpse. . . . This man has made more horrors than a lifeguard at a summer resort.

But I just saw Baron Frankenstein's latest picture and, believe me, this time he is really in trouble. When they find out he's trying to create a machine that'll take the place of a human being—he's not only attacked by a mob—but by the A.F.L.-C.I.O., the Teamsters.

And who can ever forget the immortal words of the Frankenstein monster as he stood on the tower of the burning castle while thousands of screaming townspeople threw rocks and curses and imprecations at him: "This is the way you treat tourists?"

INCOME TAX

I

APRIL 15TH: I'm gonna have to cut the show a little short tonight. Wanna leave myself enough time to fill out the income tax.

I don't wanna ruin your evening but the Government just put all the 1040 Forms into the mail. You remember the 1040 Form—Washington's way of getting you to rat on yourself?

They keep saying they're going to do something about junk mail—and yet every year those income-tax forms show up.

Into each life a little rain must fall—except in April, when Internal Revenue starts seeding the clouds.

The Internal Revenue Service is kind of a fun-type organization that solicits once a year. . . . And the basis of the whole thing is trust. All of it on our side. . . . Let's face it, we give these people billions and billions of dollars—and we don't even get a receipt!

Keep one thing in mind—they may do a lot of buck passing in Washington—but they do a lot of buck keeping too!

I think the new tax reforms are the greatest. You pay 80 per cent of your taxes in cash—and the rest in Plaid Stamps.

I bought one of those books on *How to Fill Out Your Income Tax* and they're really great. It gives you something to read while the accountant is doing it for you.

Did you hear that new LP—*The American Taxpayer Speaks?* It's a long-paying record.

We always complain about the Internal Revenue Service like it was something new. There were Internal Revenue services back in Biblical times. You remember Moses came down from Sinai

99

with two tablets? One was the Ten Commandments. The other was an expense account!

I spent the weekend reading some light fiction. My income-tax return.

Did you ever get the feeling, while making out your income tax, that the Russians aren't going to bury us—receipts are?

But I think it's nice of the Government to allow us $600 for a teen-age daughter. This covers the phone bill. Now what about her board?

I don't wanna mention any names, but I happen to know a Hollywood starlet who deducted 105 bras from her income tax. Listed them under UPKEEP.

It shows you how unfair these tax forms are. For instance, you can list your wife as a dependent, but you can't list a mistress—and they're much more expensive.

Nothing ever changes much. In the thirties, it was the Depression that kept us out of good restaurants. In the sixties, it's the Internal Revenue Service.

Boy, you could really make a fortune these days if you could come up with a product that's low-priced, habit-forming, and deductible!

Personally, I always go to a tax accountant. Tax accountant—that's a marriage counselor between you and the Government!

Did you ever get the feeling that when an employee of the Internal Revenue Service comes in to work with an upset stomach, a headache, and feeling generally out of sorts—they immediately transfer him over to the auditors' section?

Do you realize that the Internal Revenue Service is the only outfit that really knows what to give the person who has everything? An audit!

I feel every man should have at least one shabby, threadbare, worn-out suit—if nothing else, for income-tax audits.

They called one fella down for listing himself as a single man with child. They said: "This must be a misconception." He said: "You're telling me!"

And they're so subtle when they call you down for a tax audit. The Muzak is playing "Your Cheatin' Heart."

This income tax! Some people have a monkey on their back. I think I've got an eagle on mine.

You just gotta out-guts 'em! Like I once put down $4,000 expenses on a $3,000 income—and when the fella called me down, I said: "Don't bug me. I happen to be a big tipper!" And I am. I tip at subway change booths!

APRIL 15TH: I was in a bank this morning and I'll bet there are more money orders made out today than during the rest of the year combined. Everybody's standing in line with his addressed envelopes, the forms inside, the withdrawal slip, the bankbook, and the guilty look.

APRIL 16TH is the day you sit down to count your blessings— 'cause nothing else is left.

INFLATION

I don't know what's happening to prices. Meat is so high, I just bought two pounds of bacon—on the layaway plan.

For a buck and a half you don't get pork chops any more— pork chips!

Meat is so high, in Las Vegas they've now got slot machines that take hamburgers. If you hit, you get four T-bones and a lamb chop!

Prices are so ridiculous, even the butchers are getting embarrassed. I saw one with his thumb on the scale—and it was pushing up!

I've always been a little suspicious of our butcher. We call him the man with the solid gold thumb!

Last week my wife had a baby so we put it on his scale. Kid weighed 32 pounds!

Remember when $20 worth of groceries wouldn't go into the trunk of your car? Now it fits the glove compartment!

High? It's the first time I ever saw gum machines that take bills!

A lot of people feel that this is the year creeping inflation qualifies for the Olympics.

People you wouldn't give two cents for are now three for a dollar!

Times have certainly changed. Years ago you either gambled with your money or you put it in a bank. Now you can gamble with your money *by* putting it in a bank.

I'm not putting down banks, but what this country really needs is a mattress that pays 5 per cent.

People are not only spending money like there's no tomorrow— but no hereafter either! People are buying anything.
CUSTOMER: What's this?
SALESGIRL: I don't know.
CUSTOMER: In that case, I'll only take six!

The market hit a new high. Take your pick—stock, meat, or super.

INSULTS

Ain't he something? He has all the charm of a dirty Christmas card!

He has a way of making a long story short. Forgets the punch line.

I spend more than that on Tums after a Hungarian dinner!

I need you like newlyweds need the "Late Show."

I need you like a barracuda needs Polident!

I need you like Hoss Cartwright needs karate!

Lemme give you an idea what it is really like. This is the only state where bubble-gum cards are part of the Great Books series.

I notice we have a new hat-check girl this evening. Honey, whatever happened to that ugly redhead we had last week? . . . Oh, you changed your wig.

I won't say it was a cold audience, but picture two thousand Ed Sullivans!

JAPAN

I always thought the Japanese bowed so much because they were polite. Has nothing to do with it. You know under all those robes? Tight suspenders!

But it's such a lovely custom—bowing. Everybody's standing around like this: (CLASP HANDS TOGETHER IN HUMBLE BOW). Looks like elevator operators at Christmas time.

Did you ever see a Japanese baseball game? It starts at two-thirty in the afternoon when the first batter comes out of the bull pen—bows to the honorable manager. Picks up a bat—bows to the honorable bat boy. Goes up to home plate—bows to the honorable pitcher. Turns around—bows to the honorable catcher. Looks behind the catcher—bows to the honorable umpire. Puts the bat on his shoulder (TAKE BATTING STANCE) and the game is called on account of darkness.

But it's fascinating for an American to hear the Japanese manager talk to his players. You can't understand a word he says. It's like Casey Stengel over here.

And it's obvious why the Japanese have such great ball players. All you gotta do is hear the manager say: "Go to the showers—and take the sword with you!"

JUVENILE DELINQUENCY

Now there's a new government program to eliminate teen-age crime. It's called the War on Puberty.

I don't know why juvenile delinquency is called a problem. It seems to be the easiest thing they do.

I don't wanna brag but I happen to have a master plan to curb teen-age violence. We give every juvenile delinquent in the country an electric carving knife—and a two-foot cord!

But it's amazing what proper guidance will do for kids. Like I know a juvenile delinquent who used to spend all his time slashing tires. Then he got a chance to join a boys' club with a gym and for two years, he spent all of his time working out with weights, barbells, muscle developers. Now he doesn't slash tires any more—bumpers!

LATIN AMERICA

L

Did you ever get the feeling, every Latin-American country has three parties? The one in, the one out, and the third is marching on the capital . . . The whole trick in being President down there is not to expire before your term does.

In a lot of countries, being President is sort of a temporary, honorary position. It's like being a husband in Hollywood.

Castro's gotta do something about that beard. It's getting so heavy, sometimes his mouth drops open, even when he's not looking at girls.

I just found out why Playtex closed its Havana office. Too many bras were saying: "This is living?"

Wouldn't it be awful if someone put a big Band-Aid over the Panama Canal—and it healed?

LINCOLN'S BIRTHDAY

It's a strange thing they do on February 12th. Lincoln was known to have walked miles to borrow books, to get the most rudimentary form of education. So what do they do on his birthday? Close the schools!

Lincoln walked. He walked 12 miles to school—and 12 miles back home, every day. No matter rain, or sleet, or snow, or hail. No school bus. No hot lunches. Man, what a lousy P.T.A. that school must have had!

Things don't really change much. A hundred and fifty years ago, Lincoln traveled 24 miles a day to go to school. Today he'd travel 60 miles a day to go to a school with a proper ethnic balance!

It was a real problem for Lincoln to get an education. He had to do his homework on the back of a shovel. What made it a problem, it was a correspondence course!

Lincoln was so poor, he had to study by the light of a flickering fireplace. Today, you buy a house, and that fireplace alone costs $1,500!

And when Lincoln did go to class, he had to walk 12 miles to get there. Now a kid thinks he's roughing it if the school bus doesn't come up the driveway.

They called him Honest Abe 'cause as a storekeeper he once walked 3 miles to bring a woman back 6¢ in change. Sure—but what did he do with the Green Stamps?

You'll notice how they say George Washington never told a lie but they never make the same claim about Lincoln. Do you think his being a lawyer has something to do with it?

LOS ANGELES

Oh, give me a home by the side of the freeway—and let me watch the wreckers go by.

You don't know what fear is until you're going around one of those curves at 70 miles an hour—and there's a guy trying to pass you pulling a boat!

Frankly, I don't know of anywhere in California I'd want to get to as fast as these freeways can take me.

Good as they are, I wouldn't have bothered with all these freeways. I would have taken the more direct approach. Poured concrete over the whole state—then punched holes for the houses.

You have to admit Los Angeles is different. Where else can you find unemployment offices with valet parking?

The wildest things happen in this town. Yesterday somebody held up the sperm bank.

I just love the Farmer's Market. Where else can you buy bourbon-flavored peanut butter?

You know what's very chic now? Marble-top tables. You stand around drinking and it's like having a cocktail party in Forest Lawn.

I was up at Forest Lawn today. Wanted to see how the quieter half lived.

What can you really say about Forest Lawn? It's a nice place to visit but I wouldn't wanna live there.

I didn't realize how far out some of these groups are until I went to a southern California cocktail party. Have you ever tasted organically grown potato chips? . . . LSD *canapés?* . . . All-beef pork chops? . . .

M

MEDICINE

I just had a crazy thought. What if Humpty Dumpty had major medical?

This disease is so rare, they haven't even held a telethon for it!

I know a girl who's real shook up. She's been talking to this psychiatrist for five years now and the draft board just made him 4F. Hard of hearing!

I know he's a very modern psychiatrist. It's the first time I ever saw a bucket couch.

You know what bugs me? All these doctors saying you should give up smoking, drinking, overeating, and going out with fast women. As far as I can see, it doesn't do you a bit of good but you die much healthier!

Every year the Irish Sweepstakes provides Irish hospitals with millions of dollars. These are the only hospitals in the world with mink bedpans!

I wanna tell you, these hospitals swing. If you need mouth-to-mouth resuscitation, they get the best—Brigitte Bardot!

And 80 per cent of the money comes from America. Thanks to the sweepstakes, we've supported Medicare for years—only it's for Dublin.

Doesn't it bother you a little to realize we're spending $10,000,-000 for preventive medicine—but $100,000,000 for get-well cards?

They've even got a get-well card for sadists to send to masochists.

Wouldn't that be a great name for a prostate operation—a lowbotomy?

You know what bothers me about operations? Why is everybody wearing masks? . . . If something goes wrong, you don't even know who to blame!

Have you ever seen an operation? All those people standing around in green gowns and green masks and green yarmulkes. . . . Looks like an Irish Yom Kippur!

I just found out why doctors always concentrate so hard before they begin an operation. They're saying to themselves: "The ankle bone's connecta to the leg bone. The leg bone's connecta to the—"

They claim they're realistic on these medical TV shows, but where do they find those nurses? Every nurse I ever had looked like a sparring partner for (HEAVYWEIGHT CHAMP). . . . And when the patient presses the button beside the bed, instantaneously the nurse bursts through the door. This isn't even fiction—it's fantasy. Personally, I don't think any of those buzzers are hooked up. It just gives you something to diddle with while you're convalescing.

MEN'S CHARACTER

He's the kind of guy who'd put in a slug to call Dial-A-Prayer!

He's really something. This man blows his cool like Jackie Gleason asks for seconds.

I wouldn't call him insecure. Let's just say he's the type who bought an Edsel as a status symbol—and sold it for the very same reason.

Self-centered? If he was at the Last Supper—he'd worry about the calories.

This man is so inept, he isn't worrying about automation—about the Industrial Revolution!

I won't say he's chicken, but they're naming salads after him.

His idea of roughing it is cutting filet mignon with a dull knife.

Sneaky? If he were at Bunker Hill, he'd have said: "Don't fire until you see the backs of their heads!"

With his luck, he'd have founded Blue Cross during the Inquisition!

His idea of patriotism is going into a Chinese restaurant and ordering American food.

I've seen brilliant smiles but this boy gets fan mail from lighthouses!

Did you hear about the fella who was going through one of these psychological testing procedures? A psychiatrist showed him an ink blot and said: "What does it remind you of?" The fella said: "Girls!" The psychiatrist showed him another ink blot: "What does it remind you of?" The fella said: "Girls!" A third ink blot: "What does it remind you of?" "Girls!" The psychiatrist said: "All you seem to think about is sex." The guy yelled: "All *I* seem to think about is sex? Who's showing the dirty pictures?"

MEN'S CLOTHES

I want you all to be sure to come back tomorrow when my new jacket'll be delivered. Conservatively, this jacket will make Liberace look like a welfare case. . . . No sequins. No gold lamé. Eighteen thousand fireflies in heat!

I love that phrase—continental styling. What styling? It's salami casing for legs!

A salesman handed me a pair of these skinny pants and said: "It'll give you that sexy, ready-to-deliver look!" He's right. I look like a stork!

Slim? These slacks are so skinny, you gotta trim your toenails to put them on!

You can't believe how tight these pants are. One day I crossed my legs and was on the critical list for three weeks!

I found a wonderful place for continental slacks. Some of the salesmen's heels haven't touched the floor in years!

One of them takes such short steps, his corduroy jodhpurs caught fire!

MIAMI BEACH

Have you heard about the Government's new program? Federal Aid to Miami Beach? It's for all those tourists who go down there for a week saying: "Of course $500's gonna be enough!"

Do you realize there are hotels in Miami Beach charging $150 a day? Like, this might be a nice town to live in, but I wouldn't wanna visit there.

Miami isn't just a beach. It's a garbage disposal for money!

It's amazing. I've never seen so much money in circulation as in Miami. You know what they call hundred-dollar bills in Miami? Texas singles!

And everybody's getting rich. I know a bellboy who was offered the job of president of a large Miami bank—but he turned it down. Didn't want to take the cut in income!

Fair-weather friends are the ones who send you postcards from Miami.

Don't be sensitive about the weather. Think positive! Like we have the very same amount of cold as Miami does—only they have it in air-conditioning ducts.

I just got the good word from Florida. The red ball is up over the Miami Beach swimming pools. . . . Somebody could make a fortune down there with a Man Tan frostbite solution!

All you can see in Miami Beach is mink coats. Well, that's all you can ever see in Miami Beach, but now there's a reason for it.

. . . Well, I think it's mink coats. Either that or very hairy wives. . . .

Those beach hotels adapt so quickly, though. In the dining rooms, when they serve you shrimp cocktail—there's always this packed ice around it? Comes direct from the pool!

But the Miami dog track is going like gangbusters. Four speed records broken in two days. Ever since they made one change. The dogs aren't chasing a rabbit any more—a heater!

MINISKIRTS

Someone just gave me one of the new *Playboy* calendars and I was shocked. I didn't realize hems had gone that high!

These new short skirts have got the whole country hemming and hawing. The women are hemming and the men are hawing.

One Paris designer wants to raise hemlines 10 inches above the knee. But in case you're timid, he's got three different styles: 5 inches above the knee, 10 inches above the knee, and "Good morning, Judge!"

I've got only one question about these short dresses. How can you tell if they shrink?

I don't know how much higher skirts will go, but one designer said there's a definite end in view.

You know what I can't understand? Why women would want to show their knees. Who ever said wrinkles were sexy?

Remember that old saying: A man who says he goes out with a girl because of her knees—will lie about other things too!

MISSILES

These Polaris missiles are really incredible. Imagine being released from a submarine, coming up through 3,000 feet of water, shooting 30,000 feet into the air, then without a second's hesitation, heading straight for Moscow! And every night, I see people getting lost on the way to the washroom!

These are wild tests the Government is making. They send up one of our rockets—then they send up one of our missiles to shoot it down. And what does this prove? It proves if Cape Kennedy ever declares war on us, we're safe!

You know what the biggest problem is gonna be in giving up manned bombers for missiles? In 1984, no one to go to American Legion meetings!

MODERN LIVING

I've made it a point to memorize my Social Security number, my Zip Code number, and my Diner's Club number. If for no other reason than I don't like the idea of my wallet knowing more than I do.

I've lived with listening devices for years—the neighbors.

This happens to be a very memorable day in my life. I've just been notified that I am now a member of the In part of the Out group! . . . This may not seem like much to you, but it's a step in the right direction. Like getting the unlimited use of your boss's Diner's Club card—between five and eight in the morning!

All over the country, strange cults are popping up. In Chicago there's a Humphrey Bogart cult. In Los Angeles, a Peter Lorre cult. In Pasadena, a Slim Summerville cult.

There's only one problem with these Humphrey Bogart cults. How do you lisp tough?

Sometimes I wonder how Thoreau would have made out today with Walden Pond. He'd probably spend all his time fighting off developers who'd want to put up six apartment houses around it and call it an Olympic-size pool!

MODERN MUSIC

Did you ever get the feeling the human race just can't win? How else could you explain both hi-fi and rock 'n' roll coming out at the same time?

I just bought one of those $2,000 stereo sets. It not only plays 45's, 78's, and 33⅓'s—but in color!

I'll give you an idea how good this set is. The diamond needle came from Tiffany's, the tweeter from Hartz Mountain, and the woofer from the American Kennel Club!

I don't want to panic anybody, but three million electric guitars with amplifiers were given out as Christmas presents last year. This could be the end of ear drums as we know them!

There's only one problem with twelve-string guitars. When you finish tuning them, it's time to go home!

It's really amazing the way the guitar has dominated the world of music. Why when I was a kid—with Roy Rogers and Gene Autry—we never even thought of a guitar as an instrument. It was more like a weapon.

Did you hear about the rock 'n' roll singer who just washed his sideburns and can't do a thing with them?

Believe me, there's only one thing thicker than these sideburns— what's in between them!

I guess you know one of the Beatles is suffering from a very serious ailment—Receding Bangs.

I know one of these rock 'n' rollers who had a terrible experience. Right in the middle of her biggest number, she remembered the melody.

Next week we're gonna have a very unusual singing group—the Four Switchblades. They've already cut five records and a cop.

It's a very economical group 'cause they don't have to plug in their guitars. They get all their power from Beethoven spinning in his grave.

They've got a very unusual singing style. One of them loses the melody and the other three help him look for it.

Why, I can still hear them singing their inimitable version of "You Always Hurt the One You Love." And these fellas really love music!

It's the movements they go through that intrigue me—sorta like a coordinated fit.

A lot of people have been asking why they make all those funny noises and motions—and really, the answer is rather simple if you give it some thought. Consider how much all that hair must weigh—and, night and day, what it's pressing on.

Did you ever get the feeling—life was against you? Like, two years ago I wrote a song called "Hi, Dolly." Nothing!

Aren't they a wonderful group? And so religious! I think they've given up melody for Lent!

I love that record. First time I ever heard finger snapping carry the melody!

I love some of these country and western records. First time I ever heard a hog call with a beat!

I love a beat. Man, I even snap my fingers to windshield wipers!

Do you realize, if it wasn't for self-service elevators, most people today wouldn't know what good music is?

MONEY

Rich? This man even has catered icebox raids!

I know a couple who ordered $300 worth of wedding pictures and had a fight going down the aisle. But they patched it up for the sake of the photographer.

I guess you heard about the world's wealthiest fish. A barracuda that had its teeth capped.

I just read that farmers get only 2½¢ from every loaf of bread. They're lucky. I get fat.

I'm so broke, I think poverty has declared war on me!

I wish the Government wouldn't keep talking about pockets of poverty. Sounds like my pants, two minutes after my wife hangs them up.

Sometimes I get the feeling my bank balance is on Metrecal.

I won't say how little I earn, but I don't even refer to it as my pay check. It's more like a negotiable depressed area.

Each week they have printed on the check: YOUR SALARY IS YOUR BUSINESS. DON'T DISCUSS IT! Last week I wrote under it: DON'T WORRY. I'M JUST AS ASHAMED OF IT AS YOU ARE!

MOTELS

I always feel sorry for anyone with a name like Smith. It's so embarrassing registering in motels.

Have you heard about that motel that's added a resident psychiatrist to its staff? For years there have been lodging places where you press a button and someone comes up to make you feel better—but this is the first time it's ever been a doctor!

One guest had an interesting obsession. He felt people were pointing at him. No matter where he went—the coffee shop, the restaurant, the lobby, the garage—people kept pointing at him. Would you believe it? The psychiatrist cured him with one simple suggestion—tip!

MOTHER'S DAY

Let's face it, what is a home without Mother? A cheap place to go this Sunday!

This is such an important day, 'cause what would a home be without Mother? Dirty!

We had quite an interesting Mother's Day. The kids baked her a chocolate layer cake with HAPPY MOTHER'S DAY printed across the top. Only cost me $28. A dollar for the cake and $27 to clean out the typewriter.

You gotta say this about today's kids—they're unselfish. One of them just spent $10 on a Mother's Day present—two Beatles albums.

Kids are always so sentimental. On Mother's Day they pull her out of the kitchen and say: "Mom, we don't want you to do any dishes today! Leave 'em in the sink till tomorrow!"

Kids are wonderful about Mother's Day. They come up with the most wildly improbable presents—like a bottle of Midnight Passion. . . . Then they get sore when a new sibling arrives.

Mother's Day is so confusing in Hollywood, most kids play it safe out there. They send a card to their current mother, their previous mother, their original mother—and just to make sure, they also shoot one off to the costar of their father's new picture.

With each passing year, it's becoming more and more of a problem to find someone on Mother's Day who looks like one. They've all got blonde, bouffant hairdos—stacked, girdled figures—exotic make-up—a miniskirt. It's embarrassing. For Mother's Day, you don't know if you should give them candy or a talking to.

Isn't that sweet? Downtown a bar is serving martinis like Mother used to shake.

Whatever happened to the old-fashioned kind of mother—who only wanted one thing on Mother's Day—a card! And she wasn't talking about the Diner's Club.

Happy Mother's Day! This also happens to be known as Get Well Week for your friendly neighborhood candy store.

Drugstores are always on the defensive when it comes to this holiday. Notice how they keep putting up signs saying: FRESH

STOCK OF CANDY FOR MOTHER'S DAY! This means, somebody has spent the whole week tearing off Christmas wrappers and gluing on carnations!

I don't care what you say, some of the greatest actresses in this world are mothers. Year after year, it's amazing the way they can express surprise and delight over that crummy box of candy! . . . I think the only time Mom was ever surprised by that box of candy was the year it was all creams—knowing how I like caramels.

People do get some strange ideas about Mother's Day presents. Flowers and candy and perfume are fine—but who gives a Playboy Key?

This is the day, when as a big treat, you take Mom to a restaurant for food you'd complain about if she served it to you.

Mom always reacts in the same way to these restaurants. She's upset by the prices, unimpressed by the food, exhausted by the trip—but for weeks afterward, she's bragging about it to the neighbors.

And let's not forget mothers-in-law on this day either. I know, last year, I wired flowers for my mother-in-law—but something told her not to touch them.

Isn't that a wonderful title for a new mother? Chief cook and bottom washer?

MOVIE SPECTACULARS

Remember *Mutiny on the Bounty?* My wife was the technical adviser. Gave Irritability Lessons to Captain Bligh.

This picture is so long, it's a spectacle for the eyes, a revelation for the ears, and a challenge for the kidneys!

Each biblical epic starts off the same way. The Lord makes Heaven and Earth in six days and on the seventh day, He rests. If He did it today, on the seventh day He'd be doing paperwork.

And such great scenes! Noah putting two of everything into the ark. Two of everything! I think it was a government job. . . . But Noah! Noah! When you had those two cockroaches, side by side, going up the gangplank—you couldn't have gone (STAMP DOWN WITH YOUR FOOT)?

Can't you just see Noah, standing at the gangplank of the ark, as two of everything go marching by (AS IF CHECKING OFF A LIST)? "There's two elephants. Two lions. Two tigers. Two leopards. Raquel Welch."

Then there's Moses coming down from Mount Sinai. Coming down with two tablets of stone and a hernia!

Aren't you kinda glad Moses isn't alive today? I mean, how would it sound, turning to his secretary and saying: "Take a Commandment!"

It's gonna be easy to tell the atheists at these religious pictures. They're the ones necking in the balcony!

I'm always fascinated by the story of *Sodom and Gomorrah.* You might call them cities of ill repute. I'm sure you know the story. God destroys Sodom and Gomorrah but Lot's wife looks back, and turns into a pillar of salt. Which is lucky for Lot, 'cause when my wife looks back, she usually turns into another car!

I understand they made different versions of the picture, depending on which country it's shown in. For instance, in the French version, God still destroys the two cities, but he asks De Gaulle's permission first. . . . In the Russian version, God loses.

MOVIE STARS

John Wayne! This man has muscles like Jackie Gleason has chins!

Tough, rugged, always spoiling for a fight. And you can't even blame John for being mad. Look what they named him after.

Remember all those great John Wayne Westerns—with John always standing at one end of the Main Street like this? (STAND

WITH ARMS OUTSTRETCHED, READY TO DRAW.) Always stood like this. You didn't know if he was sheriff or a test pilot for underarm deodorant.

Last night I dreamt I was alone on a desert island with Raquel Welch, Sophia Loren, and Liz Taylor. No use talking. I gotta stop eating those oyster popsicles!

Can you imagine if Sophia Loren ever wanted to become a Buddhist? The troubles she'd have contemplating her navel?

Sophia Loren has said, many times, she owes her figure to spaghetti. And I see what she means. In her case, it really stacks to the ribs.

That's the wonder of Italy. How one country could turn out such small cars and big women!

No matter what happens in Vietnam, in Cuba, in Red China, in the entire world—there are still some eternal verities we can cling to. Like, Doris Day will never be the Playmate of the Month!

It's fascinating watching them make a Doris Day movie 'cause her cue cards only have one word on them: "NO!"

I had a wonderful dream last night. Brigitte Bardot came up to me and said: "I will grant you three wishes. Now, what are the other two?"

It's interesting the way the Academy Award winners come up to the platform and stammer: "I just don't have words to describe how I feel." Which is bad show business on the part of the academy. They should invite the losers up. I'll bet they'd have words.

He's the sort of celebrity, when someone drops his name, nobody bothers to pick it up again.

NEW MORALITY

N

It's amazing the way sex has dominated the American outlook. Take literature. There's *Sex and the Single Girl*, *Sex and the Single Man*. They even have a new football manual—*Sex and the Single Wing*.

Sex in college has gotten so much publicity, all over the country schools are faced with a brand-new problem—dropins!

I'm not surprised some of the fellas and girls at Berkeley are having nude parties. With those haircuts, it's the only way they can get sorted out.

It's called the free-sex movement, and so far the only thing that's right about it is the price.

Actually, these nude parties are very moral. With that big stack of clothes on the bed, who could use it?

I'm a little worried about some of these college pantie raids. It's one thing to steal panties—but some of them aren't empty!

Did you hear about the Vassar students who went on a jockey-shorts raid?

I dunno what's happening to kids. Teen-agers have always had a sex drive, but years ago they occasionally put it in neutral.

But I'll say one thing for sex in the colleges—at least parents all over the country know their kids are in bed by eleven. They don't know whose—

I didn't realize how bad it was until I found out they weren't calling them dormitories any more. Unbridled chambers!

And frankly, the kids are getting a little suspicious of all this permissiveness. They figure it might be just a sneaky way to get them to do push-ups!

But a lot of parents are worried for nothing. Like yesterday, I overheard this conversation between two college kids—and it was refreshing to hear how concerned they were over their studies:
"Sheila, I'm having a terrible time with my applied calculus. Do you think you could help me?"
"Of course I could help you, Stanley."
"Good. Your bed or mine?"

You'd be surprised how many college kids are in their fourth year and sixth month.

I don't look on (LOCAL SCHOOL) as just a college. To me, it's more like a hotbed of culture, intellectual freedom, and mononucleosis.

Have you noticed how kids seem much less inhibited these days? Now when a cop shines his light in a car—they take bows.

And cops don't ask: "What are you doing in there?" any more. Too many times they got answers.

I don't know what's happening to kids, but the progressive high school today gives three tests a semester—a mid-term, an end-term, and a Wasserman.

But isn't it sad when young people need a philosophy, motivation, and an organization—before they want to take off their clothes?

I don't wanna complain about my wife, but I think she's a Tory in the Sexual Revolution!

Personally, I don't think either side is gonna win the Sexual Revolution. Too much fraternizing with the enemy!

NEW YEAR'S EVE

New Year's Eve is sort of a target date—for throwing out the tree and 50 per cent of the toys that were under it.

Now everyone's getting ready for New Year's Eve. I know I just got in a supply of bourbon-flavored Tums.

Have you made your reservations for New Year's Eve yet? Get-well day for night-club owners? . . . You know my idea of the dumbest night-club owner in the world? Someone who goes out of business on December 30th.

You notice all the night clubs had minimums for New Year's Eve? Not one of them had a maximum?

Then you get outside at six in the morning and the car parker gets mad if you give him a half a buck—'cause he's been watching your car since last year.

Have you noticed, women never wear funny hats on New Year's Eve? I guess they figure the rest of the year is enough.

Isn't it amazing the things civilization makes us do? There isn't a river or a stream or a pond around that isn't frozen solid—but on New Year's Eve, we're still gonna be paying 75¢ a tub for three dozen ice cubes.

Now remember, at the stroke of midnight, you lean over and kiss the person in your party you love best. Then at one, after the fighting stops—

This must be New Year's Eve. All day long my liver has been cringing!

Frankly, there's only one thing more depressing than staying home on New Year's Eve—going out on New Year's Eve.

Can't you see Antony turning to Cleopatra on New Year's Eve and saying: "Just think, in fifteen seconds it'll be 32 B.C.!"

I really had a year. Nineteen sixty-nine was so good to me—I feel like sending CARE packages to Beverly Hills!

I don't wanna tell Alcoholics Anonymous how to run its business —but you know they could make a fortune selling indulgences on New Year's Eve?

I came home at four in the afternoon on New Year's Day and my wife was really steamed—'cause it was a Christmas party I came home from.

January 1st is always an awkward day. Every year there's at least two dozen sheepish-looking people with hangovers, downtown, trying to find where they parked the car.

That was a wonderful New Year's Eve party. Now if I can only get the blood out of my eyeballs and back into my veins.

What with atom bombs and H-bombs and intercontinental missiles—I'd feel a lot better about 1970 if it came with an unconditional one-year guarantee!

NEW YORK CITY

I like New York. Like Consolidated Edison, I dig this town the most!

Wouldn't it be wild if one day Consolidated Edison was digging down—and ran into a Chinese outfit digging up?

Con Edison has dug so many holes in New York, some streets don't have white lines down the middle any more—zippers!

Traffic is so clogged, what this city really needs is Dristan for streets!

Traffic is unbelievable. Somebody robbed a bank, and it's the first time I ever saw a getaway skateboard!

I happen to be the only person in America who knows the truth about Judge Crater. He isn't missing at all. He's just looking for a place to park in midtown.

People are claiming the streets of New York aren't safe, which is ridiculous. The streets are absolutely safe—it's the people on top of them who aren't safe.

Things are getting so bad, even muggers won't go out alone!

Three more incidents and they're gonna include Mugging in the Cost-of-Living Index.

But New York does go out of its way to protect tourists. Like those street maps printed on Band-Aids . . . unlimited credit at the blood bank. . . . They were also going to give out fountain pens filled with tear gas, but who could read it?

And all tourist guides warn you to stay out of Central Park—which is like Vietnam with street lights.

Central Park has the only zoo in the world where lions are kept behind bars—not for your sake but for theirs.

But it's just wonderful the way New York is going all out to make visitors feel at home. Cab drivers are grumbling much softer. . . . Parking tickets are being tied on with a bow. . . . And panhandlers have agreed to accept traveler's checks.

Have you noticed how much shrewder visitors to New York are? Like, they wouldn't even consider buying the Brooklyn Bridge—unless Green Stamps came with it.

I won't say what a rat race New York is, but where else can you buy cheese-flavored martinis?

New York happens to be a very progressive state. You can tell by the electric chair. The one with the bucket seat.

While the first Thanksgiving was going on in Massachusetts—in New York, Indians were selling Manhattan Island for $24. Just think—$24! Do you realize what would happen if those Indians looked at Manhattan today? They'd give six of it back!

Did you ever get the feeling that New York is becoming the Edsel of cities?

NEW YORK SUBWAYS

I don't have to do this for a living, you know. I could always go back to my old job—making bulletproof overalls for subway motormen!

I don't know what the crime rate on the subway is, but they just sent out for a taller graph.

After all these years, we finally know what B.M.T. stands for—Beaten, Mauled, and Throttled!

Everybody's so scared about the subways, even conductors are taking cabs!

People who want to end it all, aren't doing it with sleeping pills. With tokens!

Last week I tried to buy a life-insurance policy and they wouldn't sell me one. Claim I'm in a high-hazard category—a commuter.

Personally, I like the subway. Where else can you get bugged, hugged, and mugged at the same time?

They say the subway is the longest ride in the world for 20¢ and you better believe it! Sometimes the last stop is heaven!

I went up to a station guard and said: "What's the best way to get to Brooklyn?" So he called me a cab.

NIGHT CLUBS

I won't say the drinks in here are watered—but on New Year's Eve, this is where the police bring drunks to sober up.

You know who really deserves your sympathy on New Year's Eve? Musicians! Sitting up there on a bandstand playing "Auld Lang Syne." Do you know what it's like, at the stroke of midnight, to lean over and kiss a trombone player? . . . The suction alone is fantastic!

Good evening, ladies and gentlemen. Welcome to our tenth annual HELLO, 1970—GOOD-BY, 35 BUCKS PARTY!

I think prices for New Year's Eve parties have hit an all-time high this year. For instance, tonight—$35 a couple! Not to mention what the baby-sitter is doing to your icebox!

NEW YEAR'S DAY: Man, I don't remember when I've seen so many green complexions and bloodshot eyes. Standing up here—it's like looking in a bottle of stuffed olives.

I love the audiences we get on January 1st. I call them the salt of the earth. Jolly, fun-loving, devil-may-care-type people. Or, in the words of the psychologist—problem drinkers!

But I'll say this: In a pinch, the owners of this club are real humanitarians. Last night it got so cold in here, they started putting alcohol in the liquor! . . . Well, I guess they had to. It was so embarrassing, getting martinis on a stick.

You'll notice we have a new bartender tonight. Not that the old one did anything wrong. In fact it's just the opposite—he got religion. Started cutting the prices instead of the liquor.

Incidentally, early in the morning when you get set to leave, if any of you feel you're not in complete control of your car— please get in touch with the manager—'cause he loves to watch accidents!

It's not so bad they cut the whisky, scotch and bourbon. You expect that in a night club. But beer?

I don't wanna seem critical, but you notice how dark they keep it in here? Sure beats cleaning!

And the food! We've got the only doggie bags with ulcers!

I'm sure glad the city set a minimum age of twenty-one years for strippers. I mean, it was a little embarrassing seeing G-strings with name tapes sewn on.

I know a mink who has only one ambition in life—to own a coat made of chorus girls!

Incidentally, I understand the head of the Internal Revenue Service will be in for the last show—so the minute he comes in, I'm gonna tell soft jokes and you can talk loud business.

In conclusion, I want to remind you of one thing. If you lived in night clubs, you'd be home now!

NON-INVOLVEMENT

The newest American pastime is non-involvement. I disappear if you're in trouble and you disappear if I'm in trouble. Sort of a Mutual Fade Pact.

Suddenly the whole country is doing *High Noon* live!

Can you imagine if Paul Revere made his famous ride today? "The Red Coats are coming! The Red Coats are coming!" The only ones following him would be two dogs and an off-duty cop! . . . Not that people in 1969 are against Paul Revere. They just don't go for outside agitators.

And picture David facing Goliath, twentieth-century style—then turning to his people and saying: "Me fight him? What do we hire cops for?"

The tribes of Israel standing before the Red Sea with thousands of Egyptian soldiers bearing down on them. Moses looks up to heaven pleadingly—and a deep, sepulchral voice answers: "It's really not my affair!"

Fortunately, we still have some good Samaritans with us. Yesterday a fella was watching his wife get robbed and you could tell he was concerned. All the way through he was going: "Tsk. Tsk. Tsk. Tsk. Tsk!"

I won't say I was ignored, but I felt like a social director at an orgy.

Neglected? I get as much attention as English titles on a nudist movie.

They say the American birth rate is now the lowest in ten years—and I'm not surprised. It's all part of our new attitude. Wives all over the country are saying: "Are you coming to bed, honey?" And husbands are saying: "Please. I don't want to get involved!"

NONSENSE JOKES

Is it true the Jolly Green Giant is getting a little brown around the temples?

Personally, I've never liked morticians. All they want is my body!

This building is so high, the elevator shows movies.

Did you hear about the Method Aerialist who was killed when he did three somersaults, two twists, a back flip—but didn't reach out for the other bar? He forgot his motivation.

I gotta say one thing about my laundryman. In three years he hasn't lost a single button. Zippers, yes!

If the Administration really wants to keep the economy from overheating, it's simple. Don't let it read *Playboy!*

I really shouldn't say anything about fluoridation 'cause it really works. Yesterday I had a fluoridated martini and the hole in the olive healed up!

Now they're making a picture about a convent located in Israel. It's called: *My Yiddische Mama Superior.*

Tuscaloosa! Ain't that a wild name for a town? Sounds like an elephant with dental problems.

It must be wonderful to be a cab driver. To go to work every day in a taxi.

What do fortunetellers who use instant tea read?

Talk about secret weapons, do you know that during the last war, the enemy had a deodorant can that could spray a secret message? That's why they lost. Every time they went like this (HEIL HITLER SALUTE) we read it!

I have a great idea. We make a girdle out of $50 bills and call it a Rockefeller Foundation!

If you can build a better mousetrap, you know who will beat a path to your doorstep? Better mice!

I had a wild experience. I was walking through this supermarket and I heard this faint voice yelling: "Water! Water!" It was a package of Kool-Aid!

You keep hearing about people who can read twelve hundred words a minute. Personally, I don't believe it. Who could move their lips that fast?

I was just listening to a Salvation Army street-corner band and it was really great. One fella was singing "Onward Christian Soldiers" and his name was Ginsburg. I said: "Onward Christian Soldiers"? He said: "I'm a defector!"

Did you ever have one of those days when everything goes wrong? Like I just opened a fortune cookie and found a summons.

You know, I've never been able to figure out why it's so hard for them to find Bill Bailey. With that fine toothcomb of his, it oughta be simple. All they gotta do is look for someone with skinny dandruff!

I just had a horrible thought. You figure somewhere, Bill Bailey and Judge Crater are up to something?

I just got a crazy gift—a wind-up hi-fi.

If at first you don't succeed—better not try Russian roulette.

I just had a fantastic thought why so many American women are overweight. The glue on trading stamps—how many calories?

We get the wildest letters. Listen to this one: "Dear Sir—Last week you said some people think Hitler is still alive and living in Argentina. This is fantastic, ridiculous and couldn't happen! Signed—Pedro Schicklgruber."

Have you ever wondered how to tell a girl aspirin from a boy aspirin? If it doesn't look when it enters the bloodstream, it's a girl!

And now, for our "Famous Words of History," we take you to Coventry, England, where the next voice you will hear will be that of Lord Godiva: "Sarah's out there doing what?"

I just read a great book—*Lord of the Flies*. It's all about this fella who invents the first zipper!

What do you think paper boys aimed at before they had bushes?

NUDISM

What a dramatic moment that must have been! Eve biting into the apple, seeing Adam naked for the very first time, and saying: "This is the way you run around the house?"

Did you read about that nudist wedding? Can you imagine a hundred people standing there in the nude? Must have looked like a co-ed draft board.

You know the big problem with nudist weddings? Where do you keep the ring? . . . This can be a real problem unless you happen to carry the flag in parades.

And the words of the ceremony are kinda strange. Like: "With all my worldly goods I do thee endow." And you're standing there in your socks!

But the nicest part about a nudist wedding, you never have to ask who the best man is.

Nudist camps are places where if you see a sign saying: PUT BUTTS HERE—it isn't an ash tray, it's a bench!

OLD AGE

Did you hear about the *Playboy*-type magazine for retirement colonies? The center page doesn't fold out—it folds up!

I just heard the saddest story. About an Over 28 club that doesn't have a golf pro. It has a solitaire pro.

I think I'd be more for Medicare if they made one simple change. Based it not on how old you are, but how old you feel.

Sixty is when the biological urge slowly turns into an occasional nudge.

Let's face it. A lot of men in their sixties are heir-minded—but very few are heir-conditioned!

Then again, maybe it isn't such a bad idea having a baby at that age. You know how fathers always complain when they're asked to get up for a two o'clock feeding? If you're sixty, you have to get up anyway!

P

PACIFISM

You know what I like about pacifists? They're willing to fight for what they believe in!

I just met the world's oldest demonstrator. He doesn't want us to get out of Southeast Asia—out of Valley Forge!

One college football team has a real problem. A pacifist student got on the cheering squad and keeps yelling: "Rickety rax! Rickety rax! Negotiate! Negotiate! Negotiate!"

Did you see the new pacifist cigarette lighter? It doesn't have a wick, it has a draft card.

I've got a brother-in-law who's so non-violent, he won't even punch a time clock.

My wife is so non-violent, she couldn't hit any living thing. We've got a dog, eight years old—still goes on the carpet.

Personally, I have only one thing to say to fellas who get married to avoid the draft: Wars end!

PETS

I know a donkey with an I.Q. of 138! Hasn't got a friend in the world. 'Cause nobody likes a smart ass!

Parakeets! You think they're happy? Did you ever stop to consider what a parakeet might be thinking standing there on that perch? "Here he comes again with that 'Pretty Baby' jazz. . . . Two years I've been in this house. Haven't heard a sensible word yet! . . . The least he could do is ask me what I think of Viet-

nam. . . . And that seed! This is what they feed a growing parakeet? . . . I keep telling them, with my ulcer, I need bland
gravel!"

You think you've got troubles. I've got a canary who hangs by
his feet all day. Thinks he's a bat.

PEYTON PLACE

Have you seen "Peyton Place"—or as it's sometimes known: "A
Town Is Not a Home"?

It's the story of a small New England town that has one simple,
straightforward belief: every day in every way— That's all.
Every day in every way.

I understand it's the only community in America where the population hasn't changed in fifty years. Every time a baby is born,
some fella leaves town!

It's not exactly a mystery show, but people keep asking: "Who
done it?"

If nobody knows the troubles you've seen, you don't live in Peyton
Place!

For those of you who haven't heard of Peyton Place—it's where
Ebing learned his Krafft!

Did you hear about the girl from Peyton Place who came out
of church one Sunday after a sermon on the Ten Commandments—and said to herself: "Well, at least I've never made a
graven image!"

Is it true, as you come into Peyton Place, they have this big sign:
IF YOU LIVED HERE, YOU'D BE IN SOMEONE ELSE'S HOME NOW?

They say in Washington, politics makes strange bedfellows. Then
there's Peyton Place—where everyone makes strange bedfellows.

It's kinda hard to describe Peyton Place. It's sort of a hotbed of
hot beds!

And do you realize what these serials are doing to the housewives of America? I come home after a hard day's work feeling like World War I—and my wife's standing there in an off-the-shoulder apron feeling like Peyton Place!

The shades are drawn, the phonograph is playing soft music, martinis are on the cocktail table. And I'm shocked. I figured things like this only happened to Doris Day.

It really is embarrassing. How do you tell your wife she ought to play more basketball?

To catch up, I'm taking a portable TV set down to the office and watching the same show. Last week I went home, got off the bus, she saw me from the window, we met in the middle of the lawn. The neighbors just asked us to move.

PHYSICAL FITNESS

Have you noticed the way bus companies are doing their bit to encourage physical fitness? Every year they're stopping farther and farther away from the curb.

I just discovered a wonderful new thing—isometric karate. You break a 3-inch-thick board—by pressing on it a little each day for six months.

It's amazing how isometric exercises have caught on. There's even an Isometric Peeping Tom. Presses his nose against windows!

My idea of exercise is buying a Bobby Darin record and helping him snap fingers.

As far as I'm concerned, when it comes to physical fitness, I'm with that woman who rolled up to the Hilton in a limousine. The chauffeur gets out, picks up her eighteen-year-old son from the back seat, and carries him into the lobby. The doorman says: "Madam, I didn't know. I didn't know your son couldn't walk." And she answers: "He can walk. Knock wood; we have enough money, he doesn't have to!"

141

PIPES

You know what I love about pipe smokers? The way they always want you to smell their tobacco. I've been asked to do this so many times, I now have cancer of the right nostril!

And you're never quite sure what to say after you have smelled it—'cause what does it smell like? Tobacco, what else? . . . Behind the ears, you wouldn't wanna put it!

I know one pipe that smells so bad, it's shaped like a half-moon.

And another thing they always want to show you is their collection of pipes—especially the one shaped like Sophia Loren. No matter how you hold it, it's embarrassing.

What's the big problem about juvenile delinquency? All we gotta do is get teen-agers to smoke pipes. Who ever heard of a kid slashing tires while smoking a pipe? . . . Just keeping one lit is a two-handed job.

Do you realize pipe smokers are the busiest people on this earth? Between drawing and puffing and tamping and lighting and cleaning and knocking out the ashes—they have almost no sex life at all!

I think the only romance these fellas get is a tobacco that bites!

The greatest challenge you can give a pipe smoker is wet tobacco on a windy day.

It's fascinating to watch—the way their cheeks draw in; their stomach muscles tense; the veins stand out on their temples. I won't say what a strain it is—but with men who do their pipe smoking best—it's hernias two to one!

PLAYBOY

I just saw the latest issue of *Playboy* and it's so patriotic. It really shows the rest of the world what Americans are made of!

I was just looking at my *Playboy* calendar, and I wanna wish you all a happy January 38-24-36!

Do you realize what a great thing they've got going for them with that *Playboy* calendar? Even if they got the numbers wrong it'd be June before anyone noticed it!

Thanks to the *Playboy* calendar, it's now very easy to tell an under-sexed American. He's a person who waits till February to look at the next picture.

Have you been to the Playboy Club? I know some people disapprove of the Bunny costumes. Personally, I just look down on them.

POLITICIANS

I won't say what I think of ——'s speeches, but he'd make a wonderful neighbor for anyone with a windmill.

What do you call a presidential assistant who keeps his mouth shut? A Kool-Aide?

—— is so young, so handsome, so charming—he could be the first politician ever to turn actor.

Politicians call junkets fact-finding trips, and the fact that they find is taxpayers will stand for anything!

They fly now and we pay later!

As usual, politicians are calling for an aroused citizenry. I love that phrase—an aroused citizenry. That's what comes out of Swedish movies!

(LONG-SHOT CANDIDATE) reminds me of a fella sitting in the last row of the balcony of a burlesque show, winking at a stripper. Only he thinks he's got a chance.

One politician is using the slogan—TWO CARS IN EVERY GARAGE. Which is shrewd 'cause there's no room for them on the roads!

(POLITICIAN) has been hurt by more polls than a nearsighted dog.

They say —— has thousands of supporters. Big deal! So has B.V.D.!

It's an interesting thing the way the newspapers shorten names to three letters, like RMN. If you're a politician and your name's Sean O. Bradley—you're in trouble!

Have you noticed how politicians are always calling on God for help? And after every speech, God turns to St. Peter and says: "Man, if there's one thing I hate, it's a nudge!"

POLITICS

The President is constantly being faced with fantastically difficult decisions. Like, only yesterday he went upstairs at the White House, sighed, and said to his wife, "Honey, ask me what happened at the cabinet meeting today." She said, "What happened at the cabinet meeting today?" He said, "Don't ask!"

It's amazing how influential women have become in politics. I understand our last three candidates were picked in perfume-filled rooms.

I hope you realize some of the consequences if we had a woman in the White House. Like, every time the Cabinet met for lunch —separate checks.

Frankly, I'm not surprised that women are going into politics. Ever since the invention of Chicken Delight, they've got a lot more free time!

My wife loves to talk politics, but it's a little discouraging. 'Cause she still thinks NATO is the Green Hornet's faithful Filipino valet!

My wife is so politically unaware, she's the only one I know who can read *The Making of a President*—and not know the ending.

Do you realize the new Congress has already spoken more than two and a half million words? Two and a half million words! Sounds like the first three minutes of Jack E. Leonard's act!

If you think the days dwindle down to a precious few—you oughta see the Democrats in Washington!

You remember the Democrats—God's Unchosen People.

POPULATION EXPLOSION

India is finally doing something about cutting its birth rate. Making office parties illegal!

The population of India will double again during the next twenty years, unless something desperate is done—like bringing in TV . . . with very short commercials.

Let's face it. Many communities *are* doing something about the population explosion. There's Greenwich Village.

You think you have troubles. According to the Census Bureau, there are 3.33 persons in every American household. Just imagine how that .33 person must feel!

Believe me, the population explosion would be much less of a problem, if setting the fuse wasn't such fun!

POSITIVE THINKING

What this country needs is more positive thinking—more optimism! People have even forgotten the meaning of the word. To me, optimism is having three teen-age boys and one car.

Optimism is taking four pounds of steak, two pounds of charcoal, and one match to a picnic.

Optimism is driving a 485-horsepower sports car on the Labor Day weekend.

Optimism is your wife buying six cases of Metrecal and a bikini.

Optimism is putting aside $15,000 to build a $15,000 house.

Optimism is getting your teen-age daughter her own phone—for incoming calls only.

Optimism is buying a Mets ticket for the World Series.

In summation, optimism is pessimism—after three martinis.

POST OFFICE

Christmas is a wonderful time of the year for people who can't read or write. They all go to work for the Post Office!

I love to go to the Post Office around Christmas time. It's such a thrill watching them demolish a package just by stamping it FRAGILE!

Did you ever stop to think, between Science and the Post Office, they've got the whole world in their hands? Science has smashed the smallest item known to man—the atom! And the Post Office takes care of the rest.

I don't wanna put down the mail service, but if you really wanna find out if a toy is unbreakable—sent it by Parcel Post.

I know a woman who sent her son a Bible by Parcel Post. By the time it got to him, six of the Ten Commandments were broken!

And when it comes to deliveries, I understand the mail service was even mentioned in the Bible. It says: "The Lord made every creeping thing!"

I just came from the Post Office and it's amazing how many school teachers are moonlighting during the Christmas vacation. Someone yelled: "Where do you want this package?" Someone else said: "Here!" And two hundred teachers marked him PRESENT!

I'll never forget the first time I discovered teachers were moonlighting at the Post Office. I got a letter marked INSUFFICIENT POSTAGE—in Latin.

And they're doing the Post Office a lot of good. Why, just yesterday my wife said: "Isn't it great? For the first time, we got most of our cards before Christmas!" I said: "What's so great? They're Easter cards!"

I didn't realize how hard up the Post Office was for money until this morning. I went in to buy a $1,000 money order—and they wanted to make me a partner!

I understand the Post Office is very upset. The Russians just broke the Zip Code.

Is it true the Zip Code number for Cape Kennedy is 54321? . . . And the Zip Code number for (LOCAL DEPARTMENT STORE) is 1.98?

I know a German call girl who got put out of business because of her Zip Code number: Six? Nine! Nine!

POWER FAILURES

That's what my wife is always complaining about with me—power failure!

But wasn't it wonderful the way everybody pitched in and tried to help one another? One store owner sold me a flashlight that was a family heirloom. It must have been an heirloom. It cost $14.

Matches were going for 25¢ apiece. Used!

But thanks to this blackout, for the first time we know how the inside of a Ku Klux Klan sheet looks to a belly button!

I know a lot of people were inconvenienced when all the lights went out—but I don't think that's right, do you? Calling Thomas Alva Edison a fink?

You don't realize how dependent we are on electricity until something like this happens. I've got a sore arm from brushing my teeth!

I don't wanna shake up anybody, but when all the lights went out, I lit a match and the only thing that was going was the meter.

The TV newscasters did a great job. First time I ever saw a blackout in color!

It's obvious what caused the blackout. Five million teen-agers plugging in their guitars at the same time!

I never knew my wife was a sadist until all the lights went out. I said: "What was that?" She said: "What was what?"

I know a fella who made a fortune during the blackout—selling kerosene-operated TV sets!

In Los Angeles they don't really have to worry if the lights go out. They can always see by Dean Martin.

A waiter got so shook up, he gave me the right change!

In the Playboy Club, people were groping around for the exits. I think that's what they were groping around for.

You can imagine how one preacher felt. He said: "If I'm lying, may the good Lord strike me blind!" Then it happened.

Guilt is a fella who put a penny in the fuse box two seconds before the lights went out!

Everybody was affected—even the muggers. First time I ever saw a switchblade candle!

You can't imagine what it's like, sitting in a dark room with no radio, no hi-fi, no reading lights, no TV. I was so bored, I talked to my wife!

PROSPERITY

Economists call this an era of unprecedented prosperity. Unprecedented prosperity! That's when you can't meet the payments on a Cadillac instead of a Chevy.

Isn't it amazing the way the economy has bounced back from the recession? For a while there it looked so desperate, people were opening discount newspaper stands.

For those of you who wanna know the difference between prosperity and a recession: Prosperity is when you get the Green Stamps—and a recession is when you paste them in.

Everything's booming. Personal income is now nine hundred billion dollars a year! Nine hundred billion dollars! Where do you find a job like that? . . . I get $1.95 an hour and the leftovers from the office Christmas Party.

Employment is hitting new highs. Eighty-six million people are working. No, I'll change that. Eighty-six million people have jobs. There's a difference.

But it's the charities who really know how prosperous this country is. To get business, they now have to operate three breadlines —white, rye, and low calorie!

PROTEST SONGS

Remember the good old days—when the only song of protest was "No, No, a Thousand Times No—I'd Rather Die than Say Yes"? . . . Now they think they're gonna die if they don't! . . . Or at least get pimples.

That's the big thing with kids today—songs of protest. They're protesting poverty, atom bombs, the draft. I heard one yesterday: "Goodness Gracious, Let's Be Cautious; Army Food Just Makes Me Nauseous!"

Then there's the one on water pollution: "All the Fish in the Wide Missouri, Are Getting Drunk since They Built That Brewery!"

On detergents: "Hully Gee, Hully Gosh, Guess What Came Out in the Wash? My Fingernails!"

On international problems: "Don't Let Peaceful China Faze Ya, All They Want is Southeast Asia!"

On movies: "Busy, Busy, Busy Day; Spent It Booing Doris Day!"

On the free-speech movement: "They'll Never Call Me Hoity-toity, since I Started Talking Doity!"

On premarital sex: "Mother Says I Hadn't Oughta, so I Stayed a Virgin—Sorta."

On poverty: "Let's All Go and Help the Poor; with My Grades I'll Be One Sure!"

My wife is very social-conscious. Every time I come home, she greets me at the door with a song of protest. It goes like this: "(RASPBERRY)!"

R

RACE RELATIONS

I just heard a fascinating story. About a Negro maid who's been working for this Mississippi family for ten years—ill-treated, over-worked, underpaid—but through it all she's remained the most cheerful, happy, and contented person you've ever seen. Just by doing one thing. Every month she goes to the medicine chest in the master bedroom, finds the bottle of birth-control pills, takes the contraceptive tablets out—and puts aspirin tablets in. . . . Well, friends—her mistress is now the only mother in town with nine kids—who's never had a headache!

It's really amazing how militant the different organizations have become. Nowadays an Uncle Tom is anyone who's only been arrested once.

I won't say he's a fence-sitter, but yesterday he joined a brand-new organization—the Gray Muslims.

RADIO

Remember the Shadow—Lamont Cranston—a wealthy man about town? Why do they all have to be wealthy? Just for a change, why couldn't the Shadow be on relief?

"Tell me, Mr. Cranston, were you out looking for a job yesterday?"
"No, I wrapped myself in my cloak of invisibility and I tracked down a gang of international jewel thieves!"
"Mr. Cranston, if I had to live on $160 a month, I'd be bitter too!"

But that's what we really need—a Shadow people can identify with. A Shadow who's so poor, he has patches on his cloak of invisibility!

And a Shadow with human failings. Like becoming invisible and going into the Y.W.C.A.

Now the big thing in radio is continuous conversation. You have to be a combination disk jockey, barber, and woman!

I saw a science-fiction picture so old, the hero was inventing radio.

RED CHINA

The Red Chinese feel, if there's an atomic war, they could lose 400 million people—and still have 350 million left to carry on. I tell you—those people are all heart!

But it's very hard to think realistically about an enemy you know nothing about. Most Americans think of Red China as just one big laundry.

We have experts testifying on Red China who haven't been there in eighteen years. That's like judging Raquel Welch from her graduation picture.

We hear all kinds of solutions, but what Asia really needs is a 2,000-calorie birth-control pill!

Someone figured out that the population of Red China will increase by 250,000,000 people in the next 15 years. Personally, I don't believe it. Who could hold this many office parties?

Two hundred and fifty million new Chinese! Sounds like the only one they can say no to is us!

And somehow you just don't expect all this love-making from the Red Chinese. They're so serious, so intense, so indoctrinated with the class struggle. All I can picture is sort of a grim orgy.

These figures are even more remarkable when you see pictures of the Red Chinese women—with the fur hats, the ear flaps, the big blue coats—40-40-40! And if they take off the coat, it's even worse—15-15-15!

Now I know why they call Red China an undeveloped nation. Last week they held a beauty contest for the shapeliest figure in Peking—and nobody won. . . . It must have been a little unnerving being a judge. Like: "What are you doing after the famine?" . . . Another sneaked a pinch and broke two fingers.

One fella went with a girl for three months. Bought her candy, flowers, took her to movies. One night they went for a ride in a ricksha. Off came the fur hat. Off came the ear flaps. Off came the blue coat. It was his uncle.

I'm so scared the Chinese are gonna start trouble, you're looking at the only man in America who's hoarding pork-fried rice!

Remember the good old days? When the only problem we had in the Far East was Godzilla?

As an expert on Oriental matters, I can tell you this behavior of the Chinese is most unusual. I mean, Charlie Chan never acted this way. . . . You might question whether he ever acted at all—but never this way.

Remember those old Charlie Chan pictures? Charlie Chan was always played by a white fella and his chauffeur was always a Negro acting like a fool. All we'd have to do is show one of these pictures at the United Nations and we'd blow half the world!

Right now everybody's so bugged with the Chinese, they show Charlie Chan pictures on television and the murderer wins!

And down the street they're demonstrating against a Chinese restaurant. Pickets with big signs saying: FOO EGG YUNG!

What makes China so dangerous, it's completely unpredictable. Like a factory-second H-bomb.

Now the Red Chinese have crude nuclear bombs. What's a crude nuclear bomb? You gotta rub two sticks together to fire it?

RESTAURANTS

Boy, restaurants will do anything to get business. Out in California they've got waitresses wearing topless outfits and I'm against it. My wife couldn't believe it. She said: *"You're* against waitresses wearing topless outfits?" I said: "I sure am. It's bad enough when they put their fingers in your soup!"

But it's interesting. I was talking to the owner of one of these restaurants and he said a lot of fellas come in and even though the waitresses are wearing topless outfits, they never look up from their food. I said: "Really! Big eaters?" He said: "No. Big wives!"

And what the waitresses wear or don't wear seems to have a subliminal effect on what the customers order. As soon as they started wearing black net stockings, everybody ordered leg of lamb. Then they went to topless outfits and breast of chicken caught on. I hear one place went in for backless outfits and sold out on Parker House rolls!

Do you think this means something? A Chinese restaurant is calling Chow Mein—Liberty Noodles.

I don't understand why, but the minute they call something International Cuisine—the price doubles! . . . How much can garlic cost?

Then I asked for the check, and it's the first time I ever saw a Diner's Club card turn pale.

I just heard of a health-food restaurant that's so swank, they don't plug in a telephone at your table. An electric toothbrush!

RIOTS

Rioting is becoming a nationwide problem. This morning, eight chorus boys attacked a Y.W.C.A.!

We're having all kinds of riots. In Kansas, thirty-two corncobs attacked a farmer!

In Boston, ten copies of the *Reader's Digest* attacked a *Playboy!*

In New York, six Mets attacked the scoreboard!

In Beverly Hills, nine girdles attacked Kate Smith!

On Madison Avenue, fourteen armpits attacked a deodorant!

On Long Island, crab grass attacked a home owner!

And in Washington, all the Democrats got together to riot—but who's afraid of six people?

The looting is unbelievable. I mean, I can understand on the first night, taking the merchandise. On the second night, taking the cash register. But on the third night, coming back for the Green Stamps?

Nerve isn't going into an unguarded store and stealing a TV set. Nerve is sending in the ninety-day warranty afterward!

At least one store owner kept his sense of humor. His store was looted the first night. Then it was looted again the second night. So on the third night he put up a big sign in the window: WE GAVE!

I guess you heard about the (RIOT CITY) radio announcer who goofed? Ended a commercial with: "So why not go down to your favorite neighborhood supermarket and loot a carton today?"

I know a fella who's making a fortune. He's a glazier in (RIOT CITY).

Guts, to me, is a (RIOT CITY) storekeeper with a big front window —running an August white sale!

I'll say this. In (RIOT CITY) it's very easy to tell the moderates from the extremists. They both throw bottles, but the moderates empty them first.

I won't say how many bottles were thrown, but (RIOT CITY) is knee-deep in deposits!

"I'll have a carton of six, please."
"To take with you?"
"No. I'll throw them right here!"

(RIOT CITY) finally called in the National Guard. It had no choice. It was either bring in a thousand National Guardsmen or John Wayne!

I'm not surprised they sent the National Guard in. You know, in (RIOT CITY) an Uncle Tom is anyone who throws small bottles!

There wasn't enough troubles, the minute the newspapers called it disorganized looting, three unions got interested.

And I don't wanna accuse the newspapers of bias, but reporters keep calling it an orgy of violence—and you just show me one rioter running around naked!

You've never seen such violence. It's like a rock 'n' roll record come to life!

One committee spent five weeks investigating, took four thousand pages of testimony, and just came out with its report. That when rock-throwing, violence and looting occur—nine times out of ten you'll have a riot!

It's kinda hard to say what an investigating committee does, but if it was your wife, you'd call it nagging.

You know what (RIOT CITY) needs more than anything else? Five days of rain! Like, when have you ever seen a mob carrying umbrellas?

Everybody's talking about (RIOT CITY), but did you know there's been a riot going on downtown for the last three days? Only nobody recognizes it. They think it's the (CURRENT WILD DANCE).

I dunno what's gonna happen next. The summer's just started and already we've gone from topless bathing suits to frontless stores.

RUSSIA

Have you noticed the way the Russians copy everything we do? For instance, there will be no fraternization between males and females in Moscow University. Well—Greenwich Village has had this for years.

Actually, the biggest problem in Russia isn't keeping males and females apart. It's telling them apart. . . . This is the only country where bathrobes are considered form-fitting.

Russia has the most unusual glamour girls in the world. Some of them measure 44—in any direction. . . . And when they put on a sweater, it's like too much. All wool and a yard wide!

I got a great idea for bugging the Russians. We send them Alfred Hitchcock pictures without the last reel!

I think Russia is trying to revive the Cultural Exchange Program. Thirty-six spies are practicing the time step!

I'm not surprised the Russians are getting ahead of us. They're the only ones who don't spend half their time fighting communism!

Did you hear about the 48-26-35 Russian stripper who calls herself the Communist Front?

My idea of guts is ordering Egg Foo Yung in a Russian restaurant.

SAN FRANCISCO

You know what I like about San Francisco? It's the only town in America that wants to keep ahead of the Russians, but it wants to keep ahead of the Dodgers even more!

It's such a great thrill to be in a progressive, forward-thinking city like San Francisco. Astronauts are hurtling through the skies at 17,000 miles an hour. You're still being pulled through the streets by a rope!

Before I begin, I wanna make it clear where I stand. I'm in favor of saving the cable cars—and letting the rest of the city go!

Did you ever stop to think what you would do if you were on one of these cars and the cable snapped? I mean after that . . . It's one thing going down Hyde Street at 780 miles an hour—but what's even worse, think of that turn-around at the bottom!

SINGERS

Is that a voice? When this fella gets finished carrying a tune, you can see the fingerprints on it!

You can always tell an Italian singing cowboy. Before every number, he pulls down his bandanna and opens his shirt.

Did you hear about the opera star who does Salome entirely in the nude? Sort of a skin diva?

I don't wanna mention any names, but I know a singer who's sort of a Reverse Astronaut. He just sits there and thinks the world revolves around him.

Is that a voice? Sounds like a Rice Krispie calling to its mate!

That was Elvis Presley—the Elder Statesman of Rock 'n' Roll.

It's funny the way a song becomes identified with one person. Yesterday I found myself singing: "Bing Crosby's dreaming of a white Christmas!"

I really like Barbra Streisand—or, as some purists put it— Barbra Streisnd.

I wonder if Barbra Streisand ever feels embarrassed when she asks an orchestra to sound their A, knowing she can't reciprocate?

My wife's a real Sinatra fan. One time I said: "What's so great about Sinatra? Fellas like him are a dime a dozen!" She said: "Here's a nickel. Get me six!"

Sometime I'd like to hear the Charles Atlas people explain why Frank Sinatra is so big with women.

Is it true, if you play the Chipmunks at half speed, it's Frank Sinatra?

Did you ever hear Frank Sinatra sing? Kinda makes you want to go up to a Beatle and pull the plug out of his guitar!

I was watching Frank Sinatra on TV and a teen-ager came in. I said: "You happen to be looking at one of the finest singers in the world!" He said: "With *that* haircut?"

Which is the problem. Nowadays, sophistication is a rhinestone amplifier.

SKATEBOARDS

Skateboarding is two roller skates fastened to the bottom of a board and they don't come off. Which is more than you can say for the rider.

I won't say how dangerous skateboarding is but the C.I.A. is trying to introduce it in the Kremlin.

People worry about kids skateboarding: "How do they stop?" Not mothers. Mothers wish they'd keep going. . . . Every morning you see them wrapping the kids' lunch in road maps.

But it's great the way they do stop. Unless you're the one who's buying the shoes. . . . They may be sneakers to you but they're brake shoes to them.

You know how you can tell the champ braker? Look for a kid who plays "This Little Piggie" on his fingers.

And I guess you've heard of skateboard roulette. You pick from six places to go skateboarding in—and one of them is San Francisco.

I dunno. We never did dangerous things like that when we were kids. The worst we ever did was play bubble-gum roulette. Six kids bust their bubbles in your face—and one of them had the mumps!

SMOKING

Did you hear about the inveterate cigar smoker who had to give up playing the trombone? Before every number, he bit off the end.

You can always tell the people who are substituting candy for smoking. They're the ones who grind the wrapper out with their foot.

I can't get over the price of cigarettes. Yesterday I bought a two-week supply and I told the clerk: "I'm sorry, but all I have is a $50 bill." He said: "It's all right. You can pay me the rest to-morrow!"

Cigarettes are so expensive, I know a fella who only smokes three a day—but he stains his fingers yellow to impress the neighbors.

Incidentally, there is no truth to the rumor that the Yellow Pages are just telephone directories that smoke too much!

I won't say what it does to your wind, but you think vodka leaves you breathless? Try smoking!

What a great idea! Filter sheets for people who smoke in bed!

I'll say one thing for smoking three packs a day. It gives your hands something to do—like shake.

And there's a big crash program going on to make a synthetic tobacco from vegetables. Can't you just see yourself going into a store and saying: "Gimme a pack of asparagus—plain tip!"

Last year Americans smoked six hundred billion cigarettes! Six hundred billion! Do you realize if you placed those six hundred billion cigarettes end to end, lit the first one, and took a drag on the last one—you might have a filter that works?

Lucky Strike Green went to war and never came back. You figure it knew something?

I'll show you what I think of smoking. (TEAR A CIGARETTE IN HALF.) Now, there's one for you and one for me! (HAND ONE HALF TO RINGSIDER.)

Personally, I quit smoking—and I mean quit. No ifs, no ands, no butts!

You know who I feel sorry for? The fella who gave up smoking without any problems. But found out he was hooked on coupons!

I once had an uncle who was the sloppiest tobacco chewer who ever lived. Died of cancer of the vest!

You know what could really start trouble—science discovering a definite link between cancer and sex!

Actually, I've had no trouble giving up smoking, 'cause I just substituted something for it—candy bars. (TAKE OUT A LONG, ROUND, WRAPPED CANDY BAR, PUT IT IN YOUR MOUTH, STRIKE A MATCH, AND LIGHT IT.) . . . Man, that's real chocolate!

I haven't had a cigarette since January, and the only after-effect has been a certain dryness of the throat. Comes from your tongue hanging out!

I'll tell you why I did this. I've been smoking four packs a day for fifteen years—and I just wanted to give it up before it became a habit!

Believe me, it isn't as hard as you think to give up smoking. All you need is will power, determination, and wet matches!

I'm not alone. I know a lot of people who have sworn off. And believe me, the swearing doesn't stop there!

Naturally, you substitute other things for it. I won't say what, but I am now buying bourbon in the handy six-pack!

Believe me, there's only one way to quit smoking—cold turkey. All this jazz about 30 cigarettes one day. Then 29 the next, 28 after that. That's just flipping on the installment plan!

You know when the real crisis comes in giving up cigarettes? That first morning without one! I found myself going outside and for fifteen minutes inhaling smog!

But I gave up smoking three weeks ago and it really hasn't been so bad, 'cause I substituted something for it—shaking! . . . Really. It's been only a few weeks but already I feel stronger, more alert, more fit, more relaxed, and please, sir—don't blow it this way. I'll go out of my mind!

You know, people who give up smoking have the same problem as people spending their first day at a nudist camp—what to do with their hands.

I won't say what fifteen years of smoking has done to my lungs, but doily companies are using them for patterns.

But I must say this: Every year I have X rays taken of my lungs and the doctors never say a word. Just: "Tch, tch, tch, tch, tch!"

Just for laughs, I had my doctor send my latest chest X ray over. (HOLD UP AN X RAY.) I don't know what smoking does to the lungs but (POKE YOUR FINGER THROUGH A HOLE IN THE X RAY).

A little poem dedicated to my favorite cigarette: It isn't the cough that carries you off—it's the coffin they carry you off in!

163

People are really worried. Yesterday I saw a disk jockey playing "Two Cigarettes in the Dark" with a filter needle.

The tobacco industry is working on its first all-vegetable cigarette consisting of nothing but lettuce. In fact, that's what they're calling it: JUST LETTUCE ALONE! . . . It'll be a very unusual cigarette. It won't have a filter—mayonnaise.

For those of you who can't kick the habit, I have a great doctor who, for $75, will take your Adam's apple out and put a filter in!

Personally, I take a very fundamental attitude toward cigarettes. If God had wanted us to smoke, he would have given us chimneys!

Breathes there a man with soul so dead;
Who has never picked up a cigarette and said:
"Tomorrow, I'm gonna stop!"

I think there can be no doubt left in anyone's mind, that smoking definitely causes reports!

The Israeli Government just issued its own report and it's a shocker! Did you know that four out of five herring that smoke —get bagels?

You see what they have on every pack of cigarettes? "CAUTION— CIGARETTE SMOKING IS A HEALTH HAZARD!" Heck, so is marriage. Try coming home at three in the morning without an excuse!

Do you realize how many different industries this is gonna affect? I know one fella who jumped out of a window and he doesn't even grow tobacco. Makes ash trays!

One town is making it illegal to sell or bring in cigarettes. I figure it's gonna start a whole new industry—buttlegging!

You know, I just thought of the most dangerous thing I could do in this world? Walk through Central Park after midnight while smoking a cigarette!

Did you ever expect to see the day when people would be grateful for NO SMOKING signs?

The Ku Klux Klan is so scared, they're burning filter crosses!

They might even redesign the tax stamp that goes on the cigarette package. It won't have Hamilton's picture on it—Lucrezia Borgia's!

But I don't know if I like the idea of the Government putting down things that are no good for you. First it's smoking. What if women are next?

SOUTHEAST ASIA

This year, I didn't send my tax money to Washington. I sent it right to Vietnam. Who needs a middleman?

I can't help but have the feeling that sending ground troops to Asia is like trying to fill a bathtub with the stopper pulled out.

You know what I love? Those stories that the enemy has sophisticated antiaircraft weapons. What's a sophisticated antiaircraft weapon? A gun that reads *The New Yorker?*

I once went out with a Vietnamese girl. I think she was Vietnamese. She kept saying: "Ngo Dinh Doing!"

And these names. Can you imagine teaching spelling in Vietnam? Like it's "g" after "n" except after "y."

I feel we've got to maintain our position in the Far East. Do you realize what it would mean to lose Southeast Asia? Have you ever tried domestic litchi nuts?

Basically, there are three major groups in Washington. The Hawks, the Doves, and the largest group of them all—the Parakeets. They don't know what's going on—they just repeat everything they hear!

You know what shakes me? The way they still talk about Laos as being neutral! That's like singing "Rock of Ages" during a riot.

165

The State Department laid it on the line. It said we won't abandon our friends in Southeast Asia! I didn't know we had any.

SPACE TRAVEL

Cape Kennedy is building a supersecret project. A screwdriver with a handle 5,000 miles long—for fixing missiles with second stages that don't work.

I still can't understand why it should cost a quarter of a billion dollars to send a camera to Mars. What's it going by—cab?

Have you noticed how people are getting more blasé about these space flights all the time? Pretty soon this'll be known as taking the 9:04 out of Cape Kennedy.

Do you realize what space travel is gonna do to Metrecal? On Mars, Jackie Gleason will only weigh 40 pounds!

Do you realize we're spending four billion dollars a year just for space? Four billion dollars! There must be some way of cutting this down—like nonscheduled rockets!

We're gonna spend thirty billion dollars to find out if there's any intelligent life on Mars. Of course there's intelligent life on Mars. You can tell by the fact that they're not spending thirty billion dollars to find out about us!

The surface of Venus is supposed to be humid, steamy, and 800 degrees—which would just be impossible for life as we know it. How you gonna get Green Stamps to stick to the book?

They say the temperature on Venus is 800 degrees. What a great location for a Carvel stand!

What a landscape! Barren, desolate, no water, no vegetation. Looks just like the retirement land I bought in Arizona!

People ask: "If flying saucers are people from outer space, why don't they contact us?" Would you?

SPIES

Did you hear about the Israeli spy who joined the Egyptian Army as an undercover agent? Everything went fine until one day his whole outfit got lost in the desert—and this is what gave him away. One thousand Egyptians moaning: "Water! Water!" And him yelling: "Seltzer! Seltzer!"

Now they've got a microphone that's so small, spies can put it inside the olive in cocktails. I know the Russians are using them. Last month they got a $400 electric bill—from martinis alone!

But can you picture this scene? All over the world, spies are sitting around with earphones on listening to olives. . . . And writing down what they hear—which ain't easy. How do you spell (LOUD BURP)?

And you know who'd make a great spy for carrying secret messages? Doris Day! She's been chased in fifty-two pictures and she hasn't lost anything yet!

I love spy stories. In fact, my neighbor was just telling me about a novel in which this fella dies with a smile on his face and a hand on his hip. I said: "He's a spy?" He said: "No, a hairdresser!"

They've even got a teen-age spy and he doesn't have a silencer on his gun—he has a transistor radio. The gun still makes a noise, but you don't hear it.

One spy has a car with a shotgun in one fender, a machine gun in the other, a cannon in between—and then they put in the most dangerous weapon of them all. A woman driver!

There's even a story about a woman spy. She has long blond hair, full red lips, a gorgeous figure—and yet, there's something about her you like.

And she meets this scientist who's working on a project so secret —even Drew Pearson doesn't know about it!

167

He takes one look at this girl and goes out of his mind. He says: "Kiss me and I'll give you the plans to our new rifle!" So she kisses him. He says: "Hug me and I'll give you the plans to our new cannon!" So she hugs him. He says: "Wanna try for the atom bomb?"

But it's terrible the way these spy stories are affecting people. Yesterday I went home and my wife met me at the door. She gave me a jab in the stomach, a karate chop on the neck, grabbed hold of my arm, flipped me over her head, then she leaned over me and said: "Now, make love to me!" I said: "With what?"

I know a store detective who's fascinated by James Bond. Calls himself 006.98!

You know what I can't understand about James Bond? How he can stay at the best hotels, drive the most luxurious cars, swing with the hippest chicks in Europe—on a salary of fifteen pounds, six ounces a week . . . before taxes.

Like the way he carries on, he must spend five pounds a week for Wasserman tests alone! . . . They don't even call him a spy any more. An undercovers agent! . . . I won't say what his greatest talent is, but he'd make a great comparison shopper for Polly Adler.

The way I figure it, he's gotta be jazzing around with the expense account. Like 007 means he's licensed to kill? And so far, the only ones he's given it to are three auditors and a C.P.A.!

And he's always smoking those exotic, Middle East cigarettes. I don't know what's in them, but yesterday he flew to Turkey—got there three hours before the plane did!

SPORTS CARS

Isn't that sweet? Somebody came up with a sports car called Congress. Sounds good but it can't pass anything.

You know, in three years of buying sports cars, not once have I ever received an answer to one simple question: Who ever said sitting in a bucket was comfortable?

Say, did you hear about Jackie Gleason's new sports car? It has wash-tub seats!

Then there's the sports-car hearse. Comes with a bucket couch.

Shows you how important words are. Call it a bucket seat and it sounds romantic. Call it a pail seat and it sounds like a nudist in Alaska.

And the French are always so romantic. The French have a car that doesn't have bucket seats—it has laps!

And the Japanese sports cars are interesting. You get into them by bowing. In American sports cars, you get out of them by bowing—especially if you've misjudged where the stick shift is.

I bought one of those German cars with power brakes, power steering, power seats, power ash trays—everything's power. You don't drive it. You just sit there and tremble!

It goes 200 miles an hour! Which may not sound like too much to you, but this is in neutral!

I know a couple who had a terrible experience in a sports car. Jumped into the back seat and there wasn't any!

I just saw the smallest sports car in the world! It doesn't have tires—bagels!

SPORTS

I just read the life story of a sky diver who had one burning ambition in life—to make a round trip!

I don't wanna put down the (BASKETBALL TEAM)—but they couldn't be doing any worse if Toulouse-Lautrec was center.

FOOTBALL: I don't wanna say this team smells, but as of last Saturday they don't wear shoulder pads any more—five-day deodorant pads!

You know what skin divers are. They're surfers with a lousy sense of balance.

Did you hear about the rich surfer who has a board that sleeps six?

Say, I got a great idea for queasy surfers—dramamine-flavored beer!

What's wrong with weight lifters' wrists that they're always holding them?

You know what's very popular this year? Pool tables. One store is selling a complete poolroom kit: A pool table, six cue sticks, and a bookie.

You realize what happens when you have a pool table in your own house? You don't have a wife any more—Minnesota Fats! . . . All day long, you're out working and she's in the cellar shooting! Last night I came home starved and I said: "What's on the table?" She said: "Me. I hate to use a bridge!"

And the big craze today is a lightweight motorcycle. It doesn't even look like a motorcycle. Looks like a pregnant bicycle.

"It isn't how you play the game. It's do you win?" I have just quoted the motto of Russia, Red China, and Little League fathers.

SPRING

SPRING: when fishermen get that faraway lake in their eyes.

MAY 10TH: Today, in 1893, that famous old locomotive, the 999, went a record-breaking 112½ miles an hour. To show you how times have changed; the kid next door backs out of the driveway faster than this!

June is the month when a man making $20,000 a year feels poverty-stricken, if his next-door neighbor is putting in a pool.

Isn't this fantastic weather? The bees are buzzing, the trees are budding, and the roar of the convertible is heard throughout the land!

STOCK MARKET

So this fella walks in and finds his wife in bed with a total stranger. "What's the meaning of this?" he yells. She looks up and says: "Oh, haven't you heard? I've gone public."

I know a fella who made $10,000 in the market. He slipped on a banana peel and sued.

I had a wonderful dream last night. That 5730 wasn't just the Jewish New Year—but the Dow-Jones average!

The way it keeps hitting new highs—to investors all over the country it's the wow-JONES AVERAGE!

They say the little man is back in the stock market. What does that mean? Midgets are buying?

I don't wanna brag but I used to make $3,000 a day in the market. I was a cashier at Safeway.

People who play the stock market are fantastic. The Government announces a deficit and, right away, they wanna know who makes red ink.

And now, a word from Wall Street: "HELP!"

One day the market dropped so fast, three blue chips turned white!

I haven't been too well the last few weeks. Got hit by a falling stock market!

I won't say how I'm doing in the stock market, but if I bought A.T.&T.—that year they'd perfect telepathy!

I won't say what bad luck I've had in the stock market, but 50,000 years ago—the day they invented the wheel, I would have been investing in sledges.

With my luck, if I ever invested in General Motors—they'd bust it to Corporal!

Wall Street must feel like the Sultan in a harem. Every day it's touching new bottoms!

People aren't even calling it the stock market. It's more like Metrecal for Savings!

One investor couldn't take it. He went stock-raving mad!

Desperation is when you get a margin call from your broker and start bringing back deposit bottles!

Last year I put $5,000 into a holding company and I just found out what they're holding. My $5,000!

But you gotta look on the positive side of the stock market. Like the sound, secure investments of today—are the tax losses of tomorrow!

My impression of the end of the world: A concrete bunker 800 feet under the White House. A single individual, with a red telephone and a black button in front of him, waiting. Waiting for years. Suddenly the phone rings and with trembling hands, he picks it up to hear the voice of the President of the United States ordering him to press that button. He hangs up and slowly reaches out his index finger. But then, something makes him stop! He picks up the phone again, dials feverishly, and in a voice cracking with emotion says: "Merrill Lynch, Pierce, Fenner and Smith? Sell!"

STRIKES

As I understand it, both management and labor have agreed to a 5¢ increase. Management offered it by the hour and labor wants it by the minute.

What's really needed is a settlement that'll still leave the industry competitive—with somebody besides Tiffany.

NEWSPAPER STRIKE: Newspapers are so scarce yesterday I saw a flounder all wrapped up in the center section of *Playboy*. And you can get all wrapped up in the center section of *Playboy*. Sometimes for hours!

I'm kinda sorry to see the newspaper strike come to an end. At least it gave you a reason for being uninformed.

SUBURBIA

This town is so dull, if it wasn't for mouth-to-mouth resuscitation, there wouldn't be any romance at all!

On Saturday nights if you really wanna have a wild time—you go down to the gas station and watch them check dip sticks!

This section is so exclusive, you can't even be mugged except by appointment!

Their house is so classy, the termites burp with a broad "A"!

What the lending library is to reading, wife swapping is to Connecticut.

You know about wife swapping—the suburbs' answer to Bingo?

It's where everybody throws their keys into the middle of the room and you have such interesting experiences. Have you ever tried to make love to a Chevrolet?

I won't say how they carry on in the suburbs, but one development is calling itself Fanny Hills!

To give you an idea, you know what's the best-selling detergent out there? Mr. Dirty!

Personally, I'm against wife swapping. It's too much of a letdown when you get your real one back.

And it's so confusing for the kids 'cause they never get to see their parents. They're either away in Florida—or in California—or in Europe. A whole generation is growing up who thinks the Head of the Household is the maid!

SUMMER

I'm really looking forward to the hot weather again. When the pools, beaches, and bikinis are filled to capacity!

Can you imagine it hit 92 today and 94 yesterday? Ninety-two and 94—sounds like Met batting averages.

I guess you read about that husband who shot a lifeguard for giving his wife mouth-to-mouth resuscitation—six months after he saved her?

You know what bothers me about mouth-to-mouth resuscitation? The "re" part. Like they've been doing it before.

SUMMER CAMPS

This is the year sending your kids to a summer camp is no longer a status symbol. It's sending them to a summer camp in Europe! All morning my wife's been sewing name tapes into passports!

It's a wonderful opportunity for the kids going overseas. Now, they not only can come back with poison ivy—but typhus and leprosy too!

Naturally, some parents have little feelings of guilt at first. When they take the kids down to the airport, buy $150,000 worth of flight insurance, then look around for an old plane.

We sent our kids to a lovely little suburb of Paris last year—Camp Pigalle. . . . I won't say what it was like, but they sent us eight postcards—and Customs still has six of them!

The kids are returning from summer camp and they always come back with such an interesting wardrobe—some of it theirs.

I just got the notice from my kids' summer camps that they're gonna be open for another season. You've heard of summer camps—the T-Shirt Mafia.

These places are so lavish, you can't even call them summer camps any more. They're more like Little League Grossingers!

It's an American obsession: "Nothing is too good for my kids!" I know a camp that has two mountains! One indoors, in case it rains.

T

TEEN-AGERS

You remember Godzilla. He's big, he's mean, and he makes a mess wherever he goes. In this country he'd be called a teen-ager.

Teen-agers are very concerned about world affairs. I guess you could say it ranks somewhere in importance between Saturday night and pimples.

Like I know one student who knows just how to handle inflation, Russia, and Red China. Everything but irregular verbs.

Maybe it isn't a bad idea letting the kids take over the country. Just think, with a juvenile approach to world problems—we'd finally be able to talk to De Gaulle on his own terms.

It's amazing the changes that have taken place in dating since we were kids. Boys today are going steady even before their voices are!

Everything's upside-down. Today you gotta go steady right up to the time you get married. *Then* you play the field!

Sociologists have noted that teen-agers are beginning to swing away from sexual promiscuity and back to the sound, moral precepts of our forefathers. It's called Creeping Doris Dayism!

You can't say all these kids are bad. Why I know a fan club that just bought a Beatles wig for a bald eagle.

No question of it. Teen-agers today live the perfect life. They have an inexhaustible supply of money—Father. They have built-in maid service—Mother. They have something to take their hostilities out on—everybody. They have the final word on everything—and if you should ever prove them wrong, they look at you and say: "What do you expect? I'm only a kid!"

Do you realize that teen-agers today spend fourteen billion dollars a year? Plus another three billion that Mom slips them while Dad isn't looking?

The airlines are letting teen-agers fly for half price. It's their way of spreading juvenile delinquency evenly around the country.

I can't get over it—letting teen-agers fly for half price. How stupid can you get? They're the only ones with money!

And they never spend any of it. They're not cheap. With those tight pants, they just can't get their wallet out!

Remember the good old days, when a back-to-school sale meant pencils instead of convertibles?

TEEN-AGE APPEARANCE

One teen-ager ran away and got married, and her father took it very philosophically. He said to his wife: "Sarah, look at it this way. We haven't lost a daughter. We've gained a mirror!"

Have you noticed the way teen-agers are always looking in mirrors? Like if they ever get lost, they wanna be the first to know!

One kid logged so many hours looking into a mirror—he can now comb his hair from memory!

And those haircuts are really great if you dig mops.

I think they go into a barbershop and say: "Don't cut. Just lengthen it a little around the edges!"

I know a kid who went into absolute hysterics 'cause he lost four teeth. Not from his mouth—from his comb!

Their hair is so thick, they have a very unusual scalp problem. Not dandruff—crab grass.

You think I'm kidding, but if they ever wanted to part their hair in the middle—they'd need Moses' help!

Some people are worried about these long haircuts affecting the masculinity of teen-agers. Which is ridiculous. What's more masculine than knotty-pine pin curlers?

You know, it must be wonderful to be a teen-age girl. To be able to lose five pounds just by taking off your make-up!

TEEN-AGE CLOTHES

You know what bothers me most about the Frankenstein monster? The way kids dress today, he wouldn't even stand out! . . . Teach him how to snap his fingers and he'd be a leader!

Remember the good old days, when if you saw a slinky, sexy, seductive outfit—it was on a show girl instead of a school girl?

What about these shifts the kids are wearing? You don't know if they're in style or in trouble.

And teen-age girls are all wearing these leather boots. If you haven't seen one, picture a cuddly Heinrich Himmler.

Can you imagine going around all year wearing boots? Now you know why they scream so much—corns!

I saw one kid walking around in black leather boots with 5-inch heels and pointed toes. First time in the history of medicine, doctors have ever seen an instep with a hernia!

TEEN-AGE MUSIC

Do you realize that kids are now buying guitars at the rate of 35,000 a week? And learning how to play them at the rate of 42 a year?

The way things are going, the world won't end with a whimper, but with a twang!

Now there's a secret adult movement to do away with guitars. As the first step, they're passing out very sharp picks!

The trouble with making electric guitars so simple that a child can play them is—they do.

It shouldn't be a surprise that so many teen-agers are taking up the guitar. Isn't it the same stroke they use for slashing tires?

I was watching one of those teen-age rock 'n' roll shows and it brought to mind that old saying: "Out of the mouths of babes comes ooba, ooba, ooba, ooba, wah, wah!"

Ooba, ooba, ooba, ooba, wah, wah! That may not mean much to you, but to a teen-ager that speaks volumes. It has to speak volumes. They don't know how to read!

I know one rock 'n' roll singer who's so bad, he even snaps his fingers off key!

These rock 'n' roll audiences are really unbelievable. Picture a sit-down riot!

I don't know why they put down rock 'n' roll. You see these young kids coming out here and they're wailin' and shakin' and snappin' and quakin'! They get off this stage and they're too pooped to slash tires!

The Government's worried about the gold drain? What about the billion dollars kids spend on records each year? The scooby-doo drain?

You go into any kid's room and the first thing you see is a stack of records 2 feet high. Looks like a tall black bagel!

And every kid in the country has the same 2 feet of records—but they trade them back and forth 'cause the scratches are different.

Personally, I don't think teen-agers even like music. They're just hooked on surface noise.

And it's nowhere unless it's played top volume—on a $19.95 non-fidelity phonograph!

Believe me, if Vincent Van Gogh could hear this—off goes the other ear!

Parents are desperate. They give their kids dum-dum phonograph needles. . . . They sit around praying the holes in 45s will heal up!

According to a survey I just read, most of the records in this country are being made for the girl of twelve. And I think they're referring to her I.Q.

My teen-agers have those little transistor radios with the ear plugs, which is great. It keeps the sunlight from shining all the way through.

Now I know why they call those little records "45s." That's the I.Q. you need to enjoy them.

TELEPHONES

I have one problem with the phone company—their attitude on bills. Every time I talk to their business office, I get a Charles De Gaulle with lipstick. . . . I've won more arguments with my wife than with the phone company!

You know how at I.B.M., over every desk is a sign saying THINK? At telephone business offices, the sign says SNEER!

Have you had an argument with the phone company lately? Their answer to everything is: "The computer says—" Mark my words, someday you're gonna read about that computer—doing time in Leavenworth!

Last month I got a bill for $83. Who could talk this good? Either the bill is wrong or the parakeet's learned how to dial!

Seeing that Yellow Pages ad has given me a great idea. One-inch galoshes for people who let their fingers do the walking on rainy days!

If you've had any experience with the girls at answering services, you know anything after "hello" comes hard to them.

This direct dialing has added a brand-new ailment to the American scene: cauliflower forefinger!

The phone company may be plotting its own downfall. With all this dialing, it's getting to the point where it's easier to write.

They've even got a new long-playing record out: "Music to Direct Dial by." And it's finished before you are.

The phone company cut its long-distance rates again. Right now, they're so low, you almost feel guilty if you talk fast.

"How are you?" "Fine. And you?" "Fine. Thank you." "Good!" Now that may not mean much to you—but to the phone company it's worth eight billion dollars on long-distance calls.

I don't wanna shake any of you people who own telephone stock, but I just came up with an idea that's gonna bring coast-to-coast calls down to pennies. Two tin cans—and 3,000 miles of string!

TELEVISION

FOR SALE: Used TV set. Formerly owned by little old goldfish who only used it to watch Flipper.

Remember the good old days before TV? When prime time was any time her parents went out?

Thanks to television, kids don't climb jungle gyms any more—they watch them!

I don't mind him spending twelve hours a day in front of the TV set, but at least turn it on!

TELEVISION: our most effective pesticide for the reading bug.

TELEVISION COMMERCIALS

Let's be honest about it. What four out of five doctors really prefer, they couldn't show on television!

I'm always amused by that commercial that gets rid of a head-ache in sixty seconds—but it comes on so loud, it gives you another one.

You know what this world needs more of? Love, understanding, compromise! Like when the Bufferin meets the aspirin going into the bloodstream, why can't it say: (BOW) "After you!"

Did you hear about the headache remedy for masochists? Brings slow, slow, slow relief!

I like the commercials where they have the candid interviews: "Every time I have another baby, I get these splitting head-aches!" "Mrs. Jones, what does your husband say?" "It's Miss Jones. Why do you think I get these splitting headaches?"

Have you ever really listened to what they promise you on one of those beer commercials? It's like a bottled honeymoon!

Just got back from the beach? Stayed in the sun too long? Is your back inflamed, red, tight, and burning? Why not do what thousands of others do? Wince!

(SING) Double your pleasure, double your fun;
        In Peyton Place they ask this question: "With gum?"

A purist is anyone who hears: "Doublemint, Doublemint, Double-mint Gum." And wonders why it doesn't double your pleasure, double your fum?

People are always so excited about the new shows. How about the new commercials? Wouldn't it be great if this is the year liver bile fights back?

I was talking to a schoolteacher who agrees with that tooth-paste test. Claims half the kids in her class have holes in their heads!

I wonder if the kids who have 34 per cent more cavities could sue?

I understand the group that had 21 per cent more cavities also had 38 per cent more pregnancies. You see, without brushing they had all this time on their hands.

What this country needs is 32 per cent less cavities—but in heads!

Incidentally, I just found out how to get seventy-three shaves from the same blade—wince!

We're already starting to get the Christmas toy commercials. For $29.95 you can get a doll that walks, talks, eats, sleeps, goes out on dates, and threatens to leave home if you don't give it a bigger allowance. . . . Any more human than that and you could list it as a dependent.

Have you seen the prices on these games they advertise on television? Nine ninety-five, $19.95, $39.95! It's like Monopoly with real hotels. . . . What ever happened to those good old games like Dominoes, Old Maid, Chinese Checkers? Nationalist, of course.

It's the commercials that get to me. You know how there are some things you just don't talk about? On afternoon TV, they do!

You can't imagine the things I've found out about the lower digestive tract. I'm so impressed with this tract, if I had the money I'd build on it!

That's the gimmick. They give all these things very dignified, high-falutin' names. Like hyper-tensive gastric acidity. Ten syllables to say (BURP)!

And irregularity. I always thought irregularity was someone who came in to work late!

You know who I worry about on TV? That girl who, every time she goes to a dance, sweats! . . . And her sister keeps telling her to use a deodorant. What deodorant? Dance slower!

Did you ever wonder if Hitler got the idea for that salute while putting on underarm deodorant?

Believe me, I've got nothing against underarm deodorants. I just think there's something morally wrong in having my armpits smell better than the rest of me.

Now the big thing is spray deodorants. Every morning you stand there spraying this cold mist at yourself. Yesterday it happened. I've got the only armpit with pneumonia!

I dunno. People never used to talk about armpits until television came along. Now, thanks to commercials, it's as acceptable a subject as irregularity, slipping dentures, or postnasal drip.

I know someone who lost 28 pounds on a very simple diet. Watched three of these commercials before every meal.

These commercials get people so shook up. I know a fella who's obsessed with the idea of not offending. Every morning he gets up, takes a shower with hexachlorophine soap, washes his hair with dandruff remover, brushes his teeth with a breath-sweetening tooth paste, gargles with a germicide, drains his sinus cavities, closes his pores, squirts spray deodorant over his cream deodorant, and this man has never offended! How can he? He never gets out of the bathroom!

Be honest now. What's so terrible about offending? It hasn't hurt De Gaulle.

TELEVISION PROGRAMS

I won't say this kid is stupid, but he is the only one I know who ever flunked educational TV.

If you ask me, educational TV is a curse. My wife doesn't even have time for cleaning any more. Twelve hours a day she's in front of the tube, learning! And all over the house there are things like—Japanese flower arrangements. Dusty but exquisite!

They showed some swingin' Christmas pictures on television Christmas Day. *King Kong—Son of King Kong*—and so it shouldn't be a total loss: *King Kong Comes Home for Chanukah*.

I love that children's show with the candy cigarette sponsor. Especially when the announcer takes a drag on one of them, turns to the camera and says: "Man, that's real sugar!"

I was watching Dean Martin's TV show. It's in living bloodshot!

Dean's been having a little trouble with the commercials. One night he breathed on a spot announcement—and it came out!

And what about the program after Dean Martin? They don't know whether to call it a show or a chaser!

Remember when Milton Berle wore women's clothes, walked around on his ankles, and said: "I'll kiwll you a milyun times?" These days he could never do it on television. Too sophisticated.

The theme of TV this season seems to be the antihero. A Clark Kent who gets stuck in the phone booth!

For years television series have been made for a twelve-year old —and this is the season that asks the question: "A twelve-year-old what?"

One show is so dull it has a yawn track!

Say, if there's a ban on bombs—how come so many of them got on TV this season?

The new TV ratings came out and one producer got a .45—'cause his show got an 8.

You can tell the country's going to pot. Yesterday I was watching the "Amateur Hour." This three-year-old kid with curly hair and a dimple—sang *On the Good Ship Lollipop* with a lisp. Came in fifth!

I understand Lawrence Welk had a tragedy on his show last week. The fella who blows the bubbles lost his lip.

People say such mean things about Lawrence Welk. Like the only thing on the show that isn't square is the bubbles.

They're working on a brand-new Western TV series for next fall. The Indian medicine man isn't against the white man. He's against Medicare.

It hadda happen. This year we're gonna see television's first medical Western! The doctors will all carry hypodermics—but in holsters!

And have you watched those afternoon serials? You can't imagine the things that go on. In one scene alone there were three seductions, two orgies, and a glue-sniffing. And this was a P.T.A. meeting!

Some people think there's too much sex on television. Not me. Most of the sets are too narrow!

There's gonna be some thrilling new shows on TV this season. A modernized version of Zorro. Instead of a sword he uses an electric carving knife.

There's always one thing about situation comedies that bothers me. If the father is such an idiot, how can he support a wife, three kids, and a nine-room house in the suburbs?

Conditioned reflex is when someone turns on a situation comedy —and you get nauseous.

Aren't these TV talk shows fascinating? Did you ever figure to see the day when you'd be *listening* to Gypsy Rose Lee?

Be sure to tune in tomorrow when you'll hear a panel of housewives discuss the question: "Is your neighbor really cleaner or is she just keeping the dirt in different places?"

You know what happened to the old "Lone Ranger" television series? It's now being shown in Africa and causing all kinds of trouble. Every time the Lone Ranger puts on that mask, high priests all over the continent shake their heads and say: "This is a doctor?"

Basically, there are two types of television spy stories. The serious spy stories that get their ideas from real life. And the comedy spy stories that get their ideas from the C.I.A.

But I really shouldn't put TV down, 'cause it's just taken a tremendous step forward. For the first time in history they're considering a story about a mixed marriage—Lassie and Flipper!

I don't know what's happening to television. I really don't. I just saw a TV show in which the star was completely naked: "Flipper"!

It's a fascinating program. Every week you see a whole batch of human beings who'd be in terrible trouble if it wasn't for this big-mouth dolphin!

I don't wanna complain, but I've got a goldfish who's sat through two fires and a burglary. Nothing!

Reruns have endings you miss because your wife wants you to water the lawn—endings you've already missed because your wife wanted you to shovel the snow.

TELEVISION REPAIRMEN

I just met the world's richest man. A television repairman who moonlights as an air-conditioning repairman.

I just finished a musical about a repairman who takes six hours to fix my TV antenna. It's called: *Diddler on the Roof!*

If Bell Telephone can fix Telstar while it's 3,500 miles in the air, how come repairmen always have to take my set to the shop?

I had my friendly neighborhood TV repairman over to the house last night. He took out his diamond-studded screwdriver; twisted a few controls, and said: "That'll be $45." I said: "$45? My psychiatrist only charges me $25!" He said: "With your vertical, I'm not surprised!" . . . I said: "What could you possibly have done to warrant a $45 charge?" He said: "Three things. 1. I coagulated the circuit rectifier. 2. I goldwatered the azalea bushing. And 3. I let my wife go shopping in Saks!"

TEXAS

In Texas, it's always interesting to see what they call rivers. Up in Oregon, they've got basements with more water.

Texas rivers are so shallow, the lifeguards just know how to wade.

I've seen more water leak from cardboard ice buckets!

Playtex. Isn't that a wonderful name for a product? Of course, down in Houston it's more than a product. It's an invitation.

I'm not knocking barbecue sauce, but in Texas, if you can taste the meat, someone goofed!

Thanks to barbecue sauce, nobody ever learns how to cook in Texas. This stuff has covered up more mistakes than a maternity bridal gown!

In Texas, everything is served smothered in barbecue sauce—and that's a horrible way to go.

And I mean smothered. You order a sirloin and by the time they finish adding that sauce it looks like steak soup!

In Texas, the aspirin doesn't race the Bufferin to get into the bloodstream—to get out of the stomach!

Sometimes I wonder if they really like barbecue sauce or they're just hooked on Tums!

The first time I tried barbecue sauce I had an interesting experience. I spilled a little on my shirt. That may not sound very interesting to you, but I now have two belly buttons!

Rumor has it that Texas is now officially declared a disaster area. Not by Washington. By Duncan Hines.

This is the only state where Duncan Hines asks for volunteers!

It's one of those typical Texas ranches—with a Cadillac buckboard. . . . And the cattle aren't branded—they're engraved!

You can always tell the poor people in Texas. They're the ones who buy steak by the pound instead of by the cow.

There's a story going around about three new arrivals approaching the Pearly Gates. St. Peter looked at the first one and asked: "Where are you from?" The fella answered: "Chicago!" and St. Peter said: "You can go to hell!" Then he turned to the second and asked him where he came from, and the man said: "Los Angeles!" Again, St. Peter decreed: "And you can go to hell!" The third fella didn't even wait for the question. He said: "St. Peter, I'm from Texas. Do I go to hell too?" Peter shook his head sadly, motioned him through the gate, and said: "No, son—you've already been there."

THANKSGIVING

Thanksgiving is the day when millions of Americans finally do something about their weight. Increase it!

People who say a house is the biggest expenditure the average American family ever makes—never invited all their relatives to a Thanksgiving Dinner. . . . I don't even look on them as relatives any more. They're more like a familiar famine. . . . I won't say how big an order we placed with the A & P—but Huntington Hartford delivered it.

I didn't wanna say anything at the time, but I think we ate a sick turkey for Thanksgiving. All afternoon it had a thermometer in it.

Will power is when you go on a diet Thanksgiving Day.

Last year we had an Early American Thanksgiving Dinner. Early American. Instead of frozen food—everything came out of cans!

My wife loves to bake for Thanksgiving. She even went to baking school. Graduated with flying crullers!

I asked her: "How about making that pie that, after you eat it, you take very short steps?" She said: "What pie is that?" I said: "Mince!"

My wife makes turkey that sticks to your ribs. It takes one look at the rest of the meal and it's afraid to let go!

Girls! For roast turkey that really sticks to your ribs—baste it in peanut butter!

Somehow, our turkey always seems to last longer than anybody else's turkey. We must get the one with Platformate.

My wife has burned so many roast turkeys, Thanksgiving I'm giving her a book on bird watching.

I won't say how much I burp on Thanksgiving, but last year they had a gas war in (YOUR TOWN) and it was me!

You know what always fascinates me about the Pilgrims? Those guns they carried—with the wide muzzle. You didn't know if it was a gun or a .45-caliber plunger!

TOURISTS

There's very little difference between the tourists of today and the tourists of twenty-five years ago. They're still buying the Brooklyn Bridge only now they put it on the Diner's Club.

He travels fastest who lets his wife refold the road map.

My wife practices the Noah system of packing. Takes two of everything.

Nowadays the big travel gimmick is tours that cover 12 countries in 21 days. This is like reading every 50th word in the *Encyclopaedia Britannica*. . . . You're moving so fast, by the time you look in your guidebook to see where you are—you ain't!

One tour goes to seven countries in two weeks. What can you see in two weeks? It's like reading *Playboy* with your wife turning the pages.

I got an idea that'd increase our military strength in Europe ten times and wouldn't cost us a cent. Bring the soldiers back and arm the tourists!

The Soviet Union claims an American tourist in Russia is as safe as if he were in his own home. Only if he lives in Central Park.

It's amazing how many rich American women go to Italy each summer to feel the pinch.

Many European resorts are set up with one bath—and you share it. Sometimes with two other hotels! . . . Naturally, this calls for some resourcefulness. Like my five-day deodorant pads were giving out in six hours and forty-two minutes!

For those of you not familiar with cruises, they're Over 28 clubs with lifeboats. . . . It's like a Roman orgy where the house detectives join in. . . . Just a little different from, say, office parties. On cruises, it's the men who have to fight for their honor.

And so I leave you with this thought: "Travel broadens one!" Those famous words uttered by the first person ever to eat potato chips while reading the *National Geographic!*

TRAFFIC

Remember when we were kids? We wanted to be pilots so we could be in the Air Force, or fly an airliner from coast to coast, or explore the South Pole with Admiral Byrd. Now, kids still wanna be pilots—but it's to talk about traffic on the New Jersey Turnpike.

Over every American city today, there are ten fighter planes protecting us from the Russians—and fifty helicopters protecting us from traffic!

I figure three more helicopters and we'll need cars on the ground advising *them!*

It's really great, sitting in your car listening to them saying: "Traffic is light and moving freely"—and you haven't had your foot off the brake in fifteen minutes! . . . For him, up at 1,800 feet, it's moving freely. For you, it's a parking lot with tolls!

The way I look at it, if I'm gonna be delayed a half hour by a stalled truck in the inside lane, I don't want some big-mouth in a helicopter telling me about it! . . . Lemme find out for myself. Do I tell him his motor's on fire?

Tell me, do you ever find yourself talking back to these pilots? "Traffic is moving freely through the Holland Tunnel, huh? A

lot you know! Traffic is constipated in the Holland Tunnel! . . .
Your propeller should only be moving like this traffic is moving! . . . Don't tell me what's happening in the Holland Tunnel
from a helicopter. Get a submarine—then I'll listen!"

The Buddhist religion believes we go through a series of incarnations and during each one of these incarnations, we experience
trials, the hardships and frustrations of which make us better
people and lead us to the totality of perfection and goodness.
Now I'm not saying the (LOCAL TRAFFIC-JAMMED ROAD) is one
of these trials. . . . But if anybody wants to make it into the
world's longest shuffleboard court, he's got my vote!

U

UNIONS

SICK PAY: ill-gotten gains.

A steam shovel was digging an excavation when a union official stomped in. He said: "A hundred men could be doing that job with shovels!" The contractor agreed but added: "Why not a thousand men with teaspoons?"

A union official is someone who has only one thing against God. He worked a six day week.

As I understand it, firemen on railroads are men who do a lot of traveling that serves no real purpose. Like fact-finding committees from Congress.

These two workers are talking and one is saying: "We gotta put an end to this exploitation by the robber barons of industry, flim-flamming the workingman out of the rightful fruits of his labors. I'm going down to the union hall and vote strike!" The other one says: "Me, too! Shall we take my Cadillac or your Jaguar?"

V

VALENTINE'S DAY

My wife is a little mad 'cause I sent her the wrong card yesterday. I sent her a Valentine's Day and she wanted a Diner's Club.

I'll tell you what kind of a wife I've got. If I send her a Valentine's Day card, she claims I'm oversexed.

We don't really think about the things that we do. Like, yesterday I saw a fella buy a Valentine's Day card that says: YOU ARE MY HEART! You know what he's really doing? Calling his girl friend a red, slimy thing that goes thump, thump, thump!

I got a Valentine's Day card from my wife. It said: "Take my heart! Take my arms! Take my lips!" Which is just like her. Keeping the best part for herself!

True love is giving your wife a 5-pound heart of chocolates—and you like peanut brittle.

I like the candy boxes where you have to read a map to find the good ones. Now you can get eye strain and tooth decay at the same time!

And you hear the darnedest things in candy shops:
"I'd like a 2-pound box of chocolate-covered nuts, please."
"Cashew?"
"Gesundheit!"

And flowers are also very big on Valentine's Day. I'm giving my wife a dozen roses to match the color I always see in her hair. It's called pin-curler silver!

WAR SCARES

W

I won't say what the future of the world looks like, but it's amazing how many plowshares are being beaten back into swords!

This war scare was really the worst of them all. Let's face it, before we had only animals and human beings to worry about. Now we've got all those living bras to consider, too.

You could tell the situation was serious. A sex attack only made page 7.

There was a lot of tough talk and nothing else. We stood eyeball to eyeball with them—and they blinked like it was a contact-lens fitting!

But it's really terrible the way people start to hoard during every one of these war scares. I was in a supermarket that morning and the woman in front of me was buying 25 pounds of coffee. Isn't that awful? I was so shocked, I almost dropped my 50 pounds of sugar. . . . People do the craziest things. I know a fella who bought 400 pounds of sugar—and he drinks it black!

A lot of people started to hoard sugar and butter and meat—which is ridiculous. World War III should be a real quickie. The kind that starts at ten in the morning—so it shouldn't ruin your evening.

Suddenly, you began to wonder if history books could have a final chapter.

Fortunately, things have settled down from hysteria to our normal screaming anxiety again.

I'm just glad they settled this crisis fast. I don't think I could take rock 'n' roll war songs.

WASHINGTON'S BIRTHDAY

You know what always fascinates me? Every Washington's Birthday, all the bakeries have layer cakes with a little hatchet on top. Which is fine—but they're not cherry cakes—they're chocolate cakes. We're growing a whole generation of kids who think Washington chopped down the Hershey plant!

They say it took George Washington eight days to travel from Mount Vernon to New York. I've owned cars like that myself!

All over the East there are signs reading: GEORGE WASHINGTON SLEPT HERE. GEORGE WASHINGTON SLEPT HERE. If you think the British were worried about George, you should have seen Martha!

George Washington is the one who crossed the Delaware River at midnight and surprised the Hessians at Trenton. Which is a pretty embarrassing thing to be surprised at.

Remember that picture of George Washington crossing the Delaware? People keep asking why George was standing up in the boat. He had to stand up. Every time he sat down, someone handed him an oar!

Then came the winter of 1777. Bitter cold; people turning blue; no way to keep warm in thin, flimsy clothes. They called it Valley Forge! Today it's a week in Miami Beach!

George Washington is also known for his Farewell Address—which is surprising. It didn't have a Zip Code.

And not many people know this, but George Washington had a fantastic memory. A great memory. Why even today, all over the country there are monuments to the memory of George Washington.

WIFE

Frankly, I owe everything I have to my wife—ulcers, headaches, ticks.

My wife's been giving me the cold shoulder so much, for Christmas I'm giving her a thermal shawl.

I don't know what happens to romance after marriage, but the most I've seen in the last six months is a passionate nudge.

Before we got married she used to say: "You're only interested in one thing." Now I can't even remember what it was!

My wife is wild about the lean, hard, vicious type. I guess that's why she's so close to her mother.

I don't wanna seem critical of my wife, but I had a Bitter Lemon long before Schweppes did.

You oughta see the way she runs the kids. We're probably the only family on the block with a Resistance Movement.

Whenever my wife takes the car out for a drive, it not only ends with a bang, but a whimper too!

I'll say this for my wife—she's always willing to meet you more than halfway. Especially when she's driving.

Did you read about that woman who divorced her husband because of "habitual adultery"? I wouldn't call adultery a habit—but if it is, it sure beats nail biting!

WIFE'S APPEARANCE

I was planning to get my wife a pair of Capri pants but I don't know how big her Capri is.

Not that I'm complaining about my wife's figure. My wife has a remarkable figure—50-26-50. What makes it so remarkable—the first 50 is part of the second 50.

My wife happens to have a Volkswagen-type figure. All the weight is in the rear.

I went into a store yesterday and told the salesgirl: "I'd like to buy a pair of slacks for my wife. The kind with the funny cuffs." She said: "Bell bottom?" I said: "No, but she's getting there."

It's so hard to shop for a woman. One time I tried to buy a 6⅞ bra for my wife. The salesgirl said: "There's no such size." I said: "What do you mean there's no such size? I just measured it." She said: "6⅞? What did you use?" I said: "My hat!"

Have you noticed how most divorces start over little things? Like your wife coming out to the breakfast table in a topless bathing suit, asking: "What do you think?" And you looking up and saying: "Please! Not while I'm eating!"

I gotta be fair. My wife doesn't really dye her hair. She just touches it up—to bring out the natural highlights. And every week those natural highlights are a different color.

I once filled out a Missing Persons Report on her and when it came to the color of her hair, it was embarrassing. How do you spell "motley"?

My wife's got a real problem. She wants to have her hair dyed back to its original color—only she can't remember what it was.

I've gotten her every other laborsaving device, but I'm not buying her a dishwasher. She loses those rough, red hands—what are we gonna use to strike matches on?

I don't wanna complain but the last time I saw my wife without pin curlers was the day we got married. . . . Not that she wasn't wearing any. She just had a veil over them.

You gotta see it to believe it. Wearing high heels and pin curlers —this woman is seven feet tall. . . . She looks like a sexy radar antenna!

She's got so much metal in her hair, I'm working on a master plan. I take out $500,000 worth of insurance on her—then we go walking in thunderstorms.

And after they get their hair all wrapped up in these pin curlers —how 'bout that spray they use? I once walked into it and for two weeks my lips were glued to my nose!

WIFE BEATING

Did you read that story where it sometimes helps a marriage if you beat your wife? The family who mayhems together—stayems together!

That's right! The latest medical discovery gives us the right to beat our wives. Now all they gotta give us is the nerve.

According to three doctors, your wife may actually enjoy being beaten. 'Course, they don't say what you have to beat her *with!*

They claim many women may have a need to be beaten and that's right. You go out to Las Vegas and you'd be amazed how many of them are sitting at tables saying: "Hit me again!"

My wife has a very philosophical attitude about it. She doesn't mind my fighting with her, but she better not catch me with a sparring partner!

I think the meanest man I know is a fella who beat his wife until she was black and blue—then got a divorce 'cause she clashed with the drapes!

WIFE'S CLEANING

I don't wanna seem like a complainer, but my wife just started her spring cleaning this morning. Straightened up the mess in the living room from the New Year's Eve party.

I won't say how dirty the rug is, but when we have trouble with crab grass, it's *inside* the house!

I don't wanna complain about my wife—but on the coffee table there's a copy of *Good Housekeeping*—covered with dust.

I don't wanna complain about my wife's housekeeping, but our halls are still decked with holly.

You can't believe this woman's house cleaning. You know how husbands are always taking out the garbage? I think it's our living room they're taking it to!

We've got the only rug in town with a 6-inch pile—and I hate to say of what!

Someone came up with a new name for a wife—a Household Executive. An executive is someone who gets up late, quits early, takes two coffee breaks, a three-hour lunch, and bugs everybody in sight. You know, I married a Household Executive?

I never realized it before. I knew she wasn't just a plain ordinary housewife. I always figured she was an Uncivil Engineer!

But I can understand why a wife would wanna be called an executive. Do you realize if you had to pay for all the services your wife performs, it would cost you $30 a day? Not to mention the nights.

According to a college report, a wife's cooking and serving alone would cost $50 a week . . . $50! It's cheaper to have a girl friend and Chicken Delight!

They figure $8 a week for dusting. I wanna tell you about my wife's dusting. I'll bet you think these are gray shoes I'm wearing!

Laundry and ironing, the report figures at $15 a week. Friends, what laundry and ironing? Last month my wife went out and got me a whole new wardrobe. Even the overcoat is drip dry!

And even though everything's drip dry, she wouldn't think of washing it. Once a week I gotta put on all my clothes, fill the pockets with soap, and walk through a car wash!

The report lists dishwashing at $20 a week. Not when your wife is part of the Metrecal for Lunch Bunch. Not to mention the Sego for Supper Circle. I've eaten at home twice a day for the last six months and the only thing I've dirtied is a straw!

But I think they have something with this Household Executive bit. Let's give our wives more status, more recognition, more prestige. Anything but more money!

I'm not only gonna consider my wife a Household Executive—but I'm gonna treat her like one. When she turns fifty-five, I'm pensioning her off for a younger model!

WIFE'S COOKING

My wife happens to be very big in karate circles. You know those fellas who can break three boards with one chop? Who do you think cooks the chop?

I don't wanna complain about my wife's cooking, but yesterday she baked me a pie that looked like it missed Soupy Sales!

My wife has given me so many TV dinners, it's like a conditioned reflex. I see a piece of aluminum foil and right away I get hungry.

I've gotten so many frozen-food dinners, I send my compliments to the refrigerator!

That's all my wife knows—frozen foods. I call her Nanook of the Norge!

WIFE—MONEY

With my wife, it isn't the thought. It's the gift behind it!

I've got a wife who's obsessed with money. That's all she thinks about—money, money, money! Like last week I called her up and I said: "Honey? Did you hear the news? A space ship is going 325,000,000 miles to Mars!" She said: "Of course. If you've got money, you can travel!"

My wife believes in sharing the wealth. She shares ours with Macy's, Gimbel's, Saks.

The way I see this war on poverty—it's me and the President against my wife and her charge account.

I don't wanna complain about my wife's spending, but you are now looking at the first casualty in the war on poverty' . . . I advanced with two pay checks and an income-tax refund—and she counterattacked with two dresses and a convertible.

The government has made the first move to increase spending in the Appalachia area. They're moving my wife in tomorrow.

For those of you who don't know my wife, she's the Viet Cong of the war on poverty!

I should have been suspicious of my wife when she let me engage in premarital spending.

She has a very simple philosophy when she goes into stores— never says no. She's sort of a giftomaniac!

And she has a wonderful attitude toward money. If it costs $50 or less, she pays cash. If it costs $1,000 or less, she charges it. And if it costs more than $1,000, she rents it!

And if I say anything, she has this great answer: "It's only money!" It's only money—and she believes it, 'cause with her— money is nothing but the means to an end. And the end is Green Stamps!

I won't say how many Green Stamps she's pasted in, but last year alone she swallowed four gallons of glue!

It's embarrassing. The neighbors all think I'm a passionate lover. What passion? With those sticky lips, every time I kiss her it takes me two hours to get loose!

I wish the Government wouldn't say things like personal income rose two billion dollars a year. Now I have to convince my wife I don't make anything near that amount!

I warned my wife. One more big bill and I'm gonna flatten out her charge-a-plate!

Do you know that in Vietnam, a person can live on $15 a month? I just sent my wife!

WIGS

They say teased hair is going out. That's right. In all directions!

Two women are talking. One says to the other: "Mabel, what have you done to your hair? It looks just like a wig!" Her friend answers: "It is a wig." And the first one says: "You'd never know it!"

Wigs have really changed a woman's life. Thirty seconds after getting up, my wife is ready for any party—Tiffany on top, Bowery underneath.

Some of these wigs cost three, four, five hundred dollars—which is even more impressive when you consider the government only allows you $600 on your wife. . . . I'll take it!

Frankly, I couldn't afford to buy one for my wife. For my secretary, yes. It's deductible. . . . Charge it to Overhead.

Some of these wigs are so expensive, they've even got wig insurance. She's covered and *it's* covered!

It's fascinating watching women today in a storm. The first thing they do is take off their wig, cause their own hair is cheaper.

Some of the blond wigs are getting so realistic, I saw one with black roots.

WINTER

See? What'd I tell you? That cooler weather you prayed for back in July, finally made it!

So how does it feel to be God's frozen people?

It's fantastic how cold it is. Yesterday I saw a copy of *Playboy* on a newsstand—shivering!

You'd be surprised how many girls are wearing falsies, not for vanity—for warmth!

You know who has problems with this weather? Burlesque theaters. The girls keep getting frostbitten in the wildest places! . . . Can you imagine walking around in this weather with that little on? They must feel like call girls in a meat locker.

You know who I feel sorry for? The girls down at the (LOCAL STRIP JOINT). First time I ever saw thermal G-strings.

One girl had goose bumps so big, when she put on a bra, she had a choice!

And for the first time in years, *Playboy* is having trouble finding girls to pose. Not 'cause they're modest—'cause they're cold! . . . They hadda offer one combat pay just to get down to her snuggies.

I never figured to see so many people here during this cold wave. Shows you how many landlords aren't sending up heat!

November-December is the period of stuffing. Turkeys, people, stockings, and mailboxes.

I'll tell you what kind of a winter it's been. So far I've worn out three pairs of rubbers and one pair of shoes!

If anyone ever comes up again and tells me the winters aren't as cold as they used to be, I'm gonna hit him with the biggest thing I can find—my heating bill!

I've been taking cold medicines, pills, and sprays for years now, and I think the only temporary relief they provide is on the pressure against the sides of your wallet.

All you people who were dreaming of a white Christmas, now start working on a clear driveway!

I always thought the Abominable Snowman was a guy who charges you $5.00 to shovel off the stoop.

Believe me, frostbite is really a problem. Last week, a rock 'n' roll singer showed up at a hospital with a finger missing. The doctor said: "How in the world did you lose a finger?" The hippie said: "I dunno, man. I was standing at this bus stop—the temperature's eight below zero. I figure I'll rehearse one of my numbers while I'm waiting. So I snap my fingers like this— Ooops, there goes another one!"

Yesterday a busboy was looking out the window at the snow, turned to the boss, and said: "Ain't this fantastic weather we've been having?" The boss said: "We? Suddenly you're a partner?"

Say, if you really wanna upset your local politicians—call the money they set aside for snow removal the "Slush Fund."

Fortunately, our city has one of the most effective snow removal programs ever conceived. It's called July.

And now, a little song dedicated to my car these mornings: "I Can't Get Started with You."

I got up this morning, went out to the garage, and right away turned the car over—to the finance company. In this weather, who needs it?

My idea of guts, is the guy who just barely manages to start his car in the morning, then drives to work with the radio on.

I'll say one thing for these icy roads—they're economical. Yesterday I was doing 55 miles an hour in neutral.

Isn't that an awful feeling when you hit an icy stretch, you slam on the brakes, and all you get is exercise?

It was so cold last night, it took me forty-five minutes to get my girl friend started.

So this teacher is helping a five-year-old off with his snowshoes and says: "I guess your mother hooked these for you." And he says: "No, she bought them."

But you gotta look at the positive side of this weather. Do you realize, any day of the week you can go out to Jones Beach and find a parking space?

DECEMBER 31ST: Do you know that in 1879, Thomas A. Edison made the first public demonstration of the electric light? Not that it did him any good. It was the guy who invented the meter who made all the money.

I always get a little sentimental about January. It's the month when you're in your lowest possible tax bracket!

January is the month when the fella who told his boss at the Christmas office party, how to run his business—is looking for a new one to analyze.

The holiday season always seems to end up the same way. In December it's: "Ho! Ho! Ho!" And in January it's: "Owe! Owe! Owe!"

WOMEN'S APPEARANCE

She's a perfect 36: 12, 12, and 12. . . . I think she used to model for thermometers.

Did you hear about the high-fashion models who formed a car pool? Five in the front seat and six in the back?

Just met a lovely girl. Measures 22-44-88. Models for pyramids!

I know one girl who has a 30-40-60 figure. Goes to masquerade balls as a pear.

What would you call a German girl who measures 38-24-36? A *Stackedwurst?*

Now they're using silicone injections to make bosoms larger. One girl went up to 38 and said: "Fine!" Then she went up to 40 and said: "Great!" Then she went up to 42 and said: "Fantastic!" Then she went up to 46 and said: "Mooooo!"

You gotta wonder a little about the doctors who give these injections. I think they took the Hippo-cratic Oath.

It's really catching on. Yesterday I heard two girls singing: "Double your pleasure. Double your fun. Use silicone, silicone—"

Wouldn't that make a great name for a girl who gets these treatments? Scylla Cohen?

I dunno. I can remember when girls who measured 44 were the real thing—cotton!

I know one girl who had a terrible accident. Instead of silicone, she used that skin-tightening lotion. Where she used to be 32, she's now an excavation!

It's one thing to be fat, but when you gotta buy stretch muumuus!

It's amazing how attitudes have changed. Twenty years ago if you wanted to see a woman wearing pin curlers, you had to go to a beauty parlor. Now you just go to a supermarket on Saturday afternoon.

Women who aren't even going out on Saturday night wear them to the supermarket. So they shouldn't look unpopular.

And there's one thing that always confuses me about pin curlers. Were they named for the curlers or the heads they go on?

Lemme tell you something about this girl. If she had been Mrs. Bailey—Bill would still be home!

Did you read about that doctor in Texas who says flat-chested women have more brains than the other kind? What do you wanna bet, three falsie makers are trying to buy him off?

You know, he may be right? Every size 48 I ever met had an I.Q. to match. . . . And to make it worse, this summer, thanks to topless bathing suits, women all over the world were showing off their stupidity.

I'm not saying the bigger they are the dumber they are. Although I will say the bigger they are—the dumber they can afford to be!

But I know a fella who married a flat-chested girl for her brains and it was awful. Every morning he'd take one look at her and yell: "Quick, honey. Say something smart!"

Do you realize the full implications of this? Like, girls who measure 42 are the kind you'd like to outsmart—and can!

How about a 32 girl who wears a 42 falsie? I guess it's all right if you like dumb cotton.

Women are all shook up. They wanna know what he means by flat-chested. What's flat-chested? Friends—flat-chested is when your A Cup runneth under. . . . Then there's the Double A Cup which isn't so much a Cup as a Saucer.

If you accept this man's theory, cleavage separates the bright from the not-so-bright—not to mention one from the other. . . . Say, wouldn't that be something if there were no such thing as cleavage? Bras would be out and mail sacks would be in!

Actually, this is a very interesting area of study. Do you realize this is the only gland that operates on the Buddy System?

WOMEN'S CHARACTER

Did you ever stop to think—women haven't changed much through the years? I can see it now—25,000 years ago this caveman comes running in yelling: "Martha! Martha! I've just discovered the wheel!" And she says: "Better you should discover a dinosaur. I'm hungry!"

She's the playful type. An American at home and a Laplander at parties.

The trouble with women is, you just can't trust them. Like my wife said if I ever stayed home on a Saturday night, she'd drop dead. So last week I did—but she didn't.

She's the daredevil type of hostess. The kind who'll invite newly-weds to a come-as-you-are party.

Pure? This girl is known as the Brand X of the Bedroom!

As you know, Eve wasn't happy—although she had everything a woman could ask for. Dior fig leafs . . . heavenly Muzak . . .

no P.T.A. meetings. . . . But she wanted to eat of the tree of knowledge and she did. Whereupon she turned to Adam and said: "You only married me for my body!" Which shows you the tree worked!

She's the type who never knows what she wants until the woman next door gets it.

Don't tell me flattery doesn't work. As ye snow, so shall ye reap!

WOMEN'S CLOTHES

This season, gowns that are in, leave most of the wearer out!

The new trend is skirts 8 inches above the knee. This isn't fashion—it's nudism on the installment plan.

I didn't really believe in the War on Poverty until topless bathing suits showed me how many underprivileged there are.

I know a girl who's very upset about those topless bathing suits with just the two straps. For her this would be enough! . . . And a high-fashion model who wore a topless suit was terribly embarrassed. People kept calling her "sir."

Personally, I don't think the style is gonna catch on. I know the suits are topless but so are a lot of women! . . . And thirty years of wearing uplifts has had an effect on the rest. In one generation we've gone from Betty Boop to Betty Droop! . . . I know one woman who has such a problem, if she gave up wearing the top, she wouldn't need the bottom!

Because of topless styles, thousands of women have had their bosoms lifted. Fortunately, they were insured!

Can you imagine if the idea catches on? Beaches all over the country are gonna look like a coffee break at *Playboy!*

Wouldn't this be a great name for a topless bathing suit? "Two for the Show?"

I have only one thought on topless bathing suits. Isn't it impolite to go around pointing at people?

Topless bathing suits have really done wonders for the honesty and integrity of American womanhood. For the first time in years they're going out to the beach wearing truesies.

You know, these topless bathing suits are a problem? Did you ever figure to see the day when the only way you could tell a fella's bathing suit from a girl's bathing suit is by the zipper?

Everyone to his own taste, but if I had my choice, I'd rather see a topfull bathing suit!

Over in Europe, topless bathing suits are nothing unusual. They've even got topless and bottomless bathing suits. It's an empty box that sells for $23. . . . They don't actually describe them as topless and bottomless. They just call it a one-button suit.

It's really amazing what you see on the beaches these days. Thirty-year-old women, and they're still growing out of their bathing suits!

Can you imagine if this topless style catches on? You could make a fortune selling fat pearls to shy girls.

Frankly, I'd like to throw something over every one of those brazen hussies wearing topless bathing suits. . . . me!

I just read the saddest Dear Abby letter ever. It says: "Dear Abby: I measure 48-25-36. Should I wear a topless bathing suit?" And the answer is: "Dear Sir:"

I still can't understand why this topless bit never caught on. Women usually go for things that are 50 per cent off.

I saw one girl. Stacked? My wallet should be filled like her bikini!

Have you noticed the way bustles are making a comeback? Only they're not called bustles any more—stretch pants. . . . And if you think the pants are being stretched—you oughta see what it's doing to imaginations! . . . You can't even call them pants.

They're more like teaching machines. They outline things so clearly.

I won't say what she looked like in those tall black boots—but everybody called her the "Easy Mark of Zorro"!

I wanna tell you something about the people who make those textured stockings. Anyone who can convince women a fish net looks sexy, deserves respect!

My wife came home wearing a pair of them. She said: "What do you think?" I said: "Leave it alone. If it doesn't go away in a few days, we'll call a doctor."

She said: "It's the newest thing." I said: "So's the Hong Kong flu, but I don't go out and buy it!"

You know what really shakes you? When you see these stockings in red. It looks like diaper rash that slipped!

And have you ever run your hand along these textured stockings? It's an unbelievable sensual experience—if you're that way about gila monsters.

Believe me, patterned stockings are the greatest antimasher device women have ever come up with. I know a fella who grabbed for a girl's leg—lost two fingers on the sequins alone!

Be honest now. Take a good look at these patterned stockings. Didn't your mother used to cover the backs of chairs with them? . . . Did you ever figure to see the day when garter belts would be holding up doilies?

WORLD'S FAIR

From coast to coast, one common problem is facing the American family today—whether to send the kids through four years of college—or spend a weekend at the fair.

They've finally come up with a diet that works. You go to the fair and only eat what you can afford!

You know how to find the most popular buildings at the fair? Look for exhibits that move and lines that don't!

One line was so long, by the time I got in to see the world of tomorrow—it was!

All of the exhibitions fall into six major categories: Industrial, International, Federal, States, Transportation, and Out of Order. . . . So many things are out of order, next week they're letting tourists in free and charging repairmen.

WORLD PEACE

It may be that world peace is an insoluble problem—like two skiers making love!

The way I see it, we gotta figure out a way for (ENEMY LEADER) to save face. Either one of them.

It's hard to say where world events are leading but the latest history books list World War I, World War II, and Watch This Space!

I'm so convinced the world is coming to an end—I won't even buy five-day deodorant pads!

What worries me, is the way peace is becoming a slightly subversive concept. Yesterday I heard a politician saying: "I'm for peace!" Then when he saw he was beginning to lose his audience, added: "Not in our time, of course!"

The way the world is going, pretty soon the only Peace on Earth we're gonna have is on greeting cards.

My wife is doing her bit to bring peace to the world. Yesterday she burned her driver's license!

Every time there's trouble in the world, somebody calls the U.N. And the U.N. is finally doing something about it. They're getting an unlisted phone.

It would be great if wars could be solved at the conference table— but I've never heard of a monument to the Unknown Diplomat.